I0149099

WELFARE FAITH

For the Least of us

Kyle Raney

Urban Loft Publishers | Skyforest, CA

Welfare Faith
For the Least of Us

Copyright © 2016 Kyle Raney.
All rights reserved. No part of this book may be reproduced in any manner without prior written permission from the publisher.

Write: Permissions, Urban Loft Publishers, P.O. Box 6, Skyforest, CA, 92385.

Urban Loft Publishers
P.O. Box 6
Skyforest, CA. 92385
www.urbanloftpublishers.com

ISBN: 978-0997371727

Manufactured in the U.S.A

Editor: Stephen Burris

Graphics: Elisabeth Clevenger

Unless otherwise indicated, all Scripture quotations are from The Holy Bible, English Standard Version® (ESV®), copyright © 2001 by Crossway, a publishing ministry of Good News Publishers. Used by permission. All rights reserved.

To my beautiful wife Cassie. Thank you for excusing the terrible pickup line I used so many years ago and allowing me the opportunity to go on the greatest adventure a man could ever hope for.

TABLE OF CONTENTS

FOREWORD

In his book The Big Sort author Bill Bishop notes what we already know about our American society––we're rather migratory and seemingly rootless. However, what is notable and intriguing is that while we are more transitory than before, we're in fact clustering around others like us. Bishop writes, "As Americans have moved over the past three decades, they have clustered in communities of sameness, among people with similar ways of life, beliefs, and, in the end, politics."[1] So what does this have to do with this book in your hands?

You see, when we move to cities we end up landing places where there is religious, cultural, and political compatibility, affinity, and sameness. Interestingly, conservative evangelicals end up collecting in similar parts of the city, attending the same churches, shopping at the same stores, and spending time in social circles that overlap with one another. White, middle class, conservative, and dare I say Republican are some of the defining markers of this socio-

---

[1] Bishop, *The Big Sort*, 5.

economic religious grouping. This then sets the backdrop of what makes this book by Kyle Raney so scandalous.

Imagine living in and among this grouping as an insider but then having life throw you a curveball and you find yourself one of those ... "a freeloader, lazy, unmotivated, undisciplined, plagued with personal issues and maladies" ... on welfare. How do you break the news to others in your circle without feeling the shame of embarrassment or even the scorn of disapproval? In these circles this is a conversation [welfare] and a topic [government assistance] that is met with derision and name-calling. I see it all of the time as my social media news feed from friends and family is usually is full of articles, YouTube clips, shameful labeling, and so on related to people "not like us." Those freeloaders, those people taking advantage of the government, those lazy people who don't want to work. You see, I'm an insider too as an evangelical.

As one who teaches urban studies in college the topic of urban poverty comes up on a regular basis whether in my lectures, course reading, discussions, and so on. I have spent time looking at both the culture of poverty as well as the structure of poverty to know that labels are most often misinformed, misapplied, not helpful, harmful, myopic, and simply incorrect. Sure, there are always exceptions to everything as freeloaders can equally apply to trust fund kids. But we don't make fun of them because they drive expensive sports cars and vacation in the Caribbean.

I applaud Kyle for not only tackling this subject, but being vulnerable in sharing his own story. It is powerful. It is not only powerful because it is a story and topic that needs to be addressed to confront our own cultural biases and missteps, but it is powerful for me personally as one who has been on welfare. There is nothing more humbling than being over-educated with one doctorate while pursuing a second, working at times upwards of seven jobs at once to make ends meet, but in the end falling short. It was not from lack of effort, nor freeloading, nor the result of some kind of gross undisciplined and excessive life. Still to this day almost no one (now except you) knows that we had to go on welfare for food stamps and received free state-funded health insurance.

I get the scandal because I have lived it. When I see the rants and name-calling on my social media feed I have had to resist the temptation to quip in response wanting desperately to simply inform and educate. But usually those who lob insults via social media are also not humble nor teachable. They want affirmation, not information. Labels do not help and are hurtful and couple that together that this is a social faux pas in the religious conservative socio-economic grouping known as evangelicals and it only escalates.

What you hold in your hands just might wreck you. It may destroy your self-sufficiency as you're confronted with the scandalous gospel of grace that is transformative.

Sean Benesh

Author of Blueprints for a Just City and Exegeting the City

PREFACE

The genesis of this book started on a rainy day in Portland, Oregon, as I was sweeping the floors of my house and complaining to my wife about how I do not have time to read anymore. After spinning my sorrowful tale over how busy I am, my wife suggested that if I did not have time to read, maybe I should write. I gave a response that I think most authors probably feel on a weekly basis, "I have nothing to write about."

Fast forward a few weeks to an afternoon where my wife and I spent the day hanging out with friends who mentioned that they were going to have to go on government assistance due to a drastic and sudden change in their income flow. Our friends were scared of what others may think and what themselves would think about entering into a welfare program. That evening my wife stated, "People need to know what it's like to be on welfare and have faith that God will see them through that difficult season. Welfare is a taboo topic in our circles and it needs to be addressed. That is what you need to write about. A welfare faith." That is how this book was born and now you know whom to blame for its content.

It is becoming easier to find wonderful literature on the great need to help the poor, fight consumerism, and seek justice.[2] These books raise believers' awareness so that they may begin to reorder their priorities, step outside their societal bubble, and act on their call as disciples to seek out the welfare of others. Typically these authors wrote masterfully out of conviction, powerfully sharing their journey of fighting their idols so that they may have a greater impact on those they encounter. My intention for this work is to move a similar conversation forward, but from a slightly different perspective. My hope is that you do not glean solely the convictions of one who has failed to serve the least of these, but also to gain some perspective of what it is like to receive outside help in a social climate where those who are receiving certain types of assistance are often looked down upon.

My aim is to simply tell our family's story of how we survived going on government assistance and how the results of that season made us more intentional followers of Christ. It is my hope to give some insight into what it is like to be a believer in Christ who enters into a government-funded program that many in the church feel is a waste of our country's revenue. Something has happened to our collective Christian conscience where we have become too political and/or judgmental about

---

[2] A few of my favorites: Shane Claiborne, *The Irresistible Revolution*; Jen Hatmaker, *Seven*; Brandon Hatmaker, *Barefoot Church*; David Platt, *Radical*, just to name a few.

welfare and other social issues to the detriment of our gospel witness. Whether it's getting upset during the holidays with companies that are removing any reference to Christmas from their stores or the battle to save America from particular cultural influences, it is starting to feel like we exerting a ton of effort in the wrong fight.

Welfare Faith is not meant to malign Christians, but to possibly prompt the reader to have the same honest conversations I had with Jesus regarding His interests in my welfare, as well as, my lack of concern with the welfare of others. *Welfare Faith* is not meant to be an academic work, a political agenda piece, or an emotional barrage on the reader's conscience. I am simply a storyteller who understands that others have gone through much worse, but who still feels my family's story could be of value to some who call themselves Christians. Finally, I wanted to give an albeit small and brief voice to those who are on government assistance and let a portion of their side of the story be heard in hopes that it creates a healthier insight to all who follow Jesus.

ACKNOWLEDGMENTS

I want to say a special thank you to Dr. Sean Benesh and Urban Loft Publishing for rolling the dice on this book. Thank you for expanding your vision for storytellers and allowing me a platform for my reflections. Thank you to my family and friends who allowed me the time to stop writing at different moments over the past year so I could remember why I took on this project in the first place. Finally, thank you to all who have faced similar trials, stood tall in the midst of storms, and unknowingly became the inspiration of so many of these pages.

INTRODUCTION

There are several biblical and theological positions we adopt when we become believers in Christ. There are certain rhythms we accept, attitudes we assume, and particular stances we are asked to take on for the glory of God. We are ushered into this new and diverse family called the church where at times the only commonality we find with one another is that we all needed Christ to make us whole again. We are changed for the better and now find ourselves living counter to the culture we once knew.

Within this new circle of Jesus-loving people we are also introduced to beliefs and/or habits in which the evangelical culture has also asked us to adhere to, even though some of these principles or actions may be hard to trace back to Scripture. We find these extra-biblical positions surface in the voting booth, media outlets, and in our cultural circles. Every year we are witnessing an ever-greater separation occurring between Christians and culture. This expanding separation is troubling since we are mandated by Scripture to engage the very same culture that some us of are avoiding with our newfound faith.[3]

For quite some time now Christians have begun to form metaphorical islands of the like-minded to land upon where they may feel more comfortable and better able to avoid the choppy waves of secularism. When we are on these islands, it becomes easier to lob complaints, fears, and accusations towards situations and certain people groups. If someone on these mythical islands of ideas dares to wade into the waters of the world, even while wearing the life-vest of the gospel, we are quick to abandon them to the sharks of society for having "sold out" or "turned their back" on the truth.

What would it be like to build boats in order that we may leave these islands of opinions, and experience first-hand what it is like to be amongst those who are lost in a sea of the unknown? We may find some people floating by who we can tell about our boat and how it can change their situation. Some of the people in our boats may go overboard, but they have shipmates who can help them back into the safety of their grace-filled vessel. The islands would begin to move to the distant horizon and together we would seek out future passengers who would join us on a journey that ultimately leads to an eternity with God.

Many evangelicals formulate more of their opinions from news sources or Christian talking heads, rather than from God's Word. When this happens, groupthink can occur and unhelpful stereotypes can form. Not only does this impact our

---

[3] Psalm 96:3; Mark 16:15; Romans 10:13-15; 1 Corinthians 9:22

worldview, but it also affects how we minister to those in our community. If we are not careful, the caricatures that surface regarding certain groups of people may not just thwart our desires to love and serve them, but also cause us to fall into sin. People of different cultural backgrounds, social lifestyles, and political leanings are just a few of the groups that a portion of the church is isolating. However, if we have to start somewhere, welfare recipients is not a bad place to begin the conversation of how to look past someone's outward situation in order to seek out their well-being thus resembling what Christ has done for us.

Debating the structure, effectiveness, and future of our welfare system is a great conversation, but not one that this book will engage in. Overloading the reader with opinions, statistics, and political rhetoric are not my goals. Rather I would like to speak to the attitude of the believer in regards to those who are on welfare and to people in general who may not completely embody the modern evangelical. At least in my case, what I found was not pretty, but I needed to see the disenfranchisement of my own heart before it could begin to heal. After my family's experience on welfare we realized it may be time to get off the island and go seek out better shores.

CHAPTER 1

Deep Breath

I live on a small four-acre farm at the edge of Portland, Oregon. I was told once that technically it's not a farm because nothing grows on the property other than weeds. However, this came from a native hipster who only grows ironic mustaches. That's how this city works. In Portland you can find yourself surrounded by a beautiful forest of evergreen trees and still hear the sounds of a local Indie band or smell the latest creation from a food cart that is ready to serve the hungry masses. Many who live outside of Portland believe that our city feels more like a foreign country, but they are mistaken. Our fair city should be classified as its own planet and that is just the way we like it.

After my six kids fall asleep I often take walks on our property in order to just breathe. Not the type of breathing that we unconsciously do every few seconds of our lives, but the type of breathing that our soul participates in where, for a few fleeting moments, everything feels right with the world. If I had neighbors close by they would think I was crazy because more than once I have found myself in a trance, staring at the forest that surrounds our property and trying to comprehend the complexities of God's creation. In these moments my mind is quieted, time has slowed to a crawl, and hope sets profoundly rooted within my spirit. The deep "soul breaths" are long and poetic, leading my mind to be inspired about what we can achieve and wondering what we have yet to experience.

There was a time I felt that I would never take one of these "breaths" again. Trials in life have the ability to knock the wind right out of our chest and suffocate any hope we may try to muster. We can do our best to isolate ourselves from the pain, but trials have ways of finding us no matter where we choose to hide. The difficult times can be terrible, but I never feel more vulnerable, more finite, more dependent, or more human than when enduring hardships.

Trials are often referred to as storms. Some we can see brewing miles away and others hit us out of nowhere finding us unprepared, exposed, and vulnerable to their havoc. We are often unwilling participants in these situations that will either forge our resolve or cultivate our despair. In the midst of these course-altering events there are usually moments of revelation that crash down upon us where we realize that we are not as invincible as we thought, and that if we are not careful, this season of difficulty could lead to brokenness that lasts a life-time.

My story is not about addiction, the loss of a loved one, or some physical obstacle that I had to overcome. Many would see my family's storm as a quiet rustling of the wind and not a great squall of tragedy. However, it was an unexpected and humbling turn of events nonetheless that came packaged in a small plastic card that told the world the Raney family was now on welfare...and the struggle to breathe began.

It felt as if I was living some sad narrative you might see on a daytime TV movie. I was a 30-year-old pastor with young children and a charming wife fighting off the whims of poverty. My dream to impact the lives of other people faded as I stared at a glistening white Supplemental Nutrition Assistance Program (SNAP) card that served as a beacon of failure, warning passersby to stand back in case poverty was contagious. Young adults at my stage of life were not typically rummaging through their pay stubs in order to prove to the government that they were poor, but I soon became an expert at this sport of the economically disadvantaged.

A few years ago my wife Cassie and I leapt blindly into the church-planting surge that was reshaping many sectors of evangelicalism. We had served previously in student ministry in Oklahoma, but knew in our hearts that starting new churches is where God desired our efforts. We packed our bags, crossed the Red River, and headed back to our home state of Texas in order to start a new church in Fort Worth.

During the transition from mega-church staffer to church planter, I began to develop a debilitating ego where I was convinced that my efforts were going to fix every problem that plagued Christendom (which seemed like a healthy goal at the time). I found myself in a world of cynicism justified by "righteous" frustrations that I had accumulated over the years. It was not that I had served in bad churches; it was the fact that I was trying to fit into a system which my gifts were not suited for. Instead of realizing that I was the problem, I instead saw every other church that did not match my philosophy as the problem.

As if church planting as an egomaniac did not provide its challenges, I was also struggling to find enough work as a part-time college instructor to support my family. I just assumed people would love me as much I loved myself and swoon over my abilities to teach the next generation the wisdom they so desperately needed! I was an adjunct instructor without the students that typically would pay good money to fall asleep in my class.

Let me take a slight detour to speak about the profession of an adjunct or part-time educator. Whether you are a substitute for a local school district or working as an adjunct instructor at institutions of higher learning, ultimately you are a teaching hustler trying to gain as many classes as you can at whatever institution (reputable or not) that will take you on. The problem is that work is never guaranteed. Your fate as an adjunct instructor does not rely on your ability to teach, but on 18-20 year-old college students who will decide whether your class seems worth taking or not. If you do not have enough students signed up for the class, then the class is terminated faster than you can say "health and human services."

In the second year of church planting, both of the schools I was working for had offered me classes, but right before the semester was to begin, most of these courses did not make the cut because... well, who really wants to take "Introduction to Local Government" anyway? My vocational revenue stream fell apart thus forcing the first domino of our welfare adventure to fall. I had raised financial support in order to help sustain my family while starting a new church, but over time, other than a few supporters who had continued to give, the money simply stopped coming in. My lack of employment and fading resources led my family to embrace the world of government assistance where humility is found at every turn. Suffocation had commenced.

Experiencing a life on government assistance was never a goal that I hoped to achieve. I did not sit in my high school counselor's office in south Houston and let her in on some duplicitous plan to someday live off the compulsory giving of others. Under my yearbook picture the caption did not read, "Most likely to be co-dependent." I do not know anyone who would actually orchestrate situations in their lives that would force them to seek outside assistance in order to survive. There is a natural characteristic built within the makeup of humans to seek stability, but too often that stability is concentrated in the accumulation of material things. It is when life removes these bastions of material stability that we so often find ourselves scrambling to find hope; grasping to be anchored to something greater than our situation.

The desire to be successful is heightened within the United States due to the euphoric nature of the American Dream. The rags-to-riches fantasy is engrained in every aspect of our society, projecting a message that if you cannot make it here, then you cannot make it in life. Pastors are not immune to these desires and many will do whatever it takes to become successful in the eyes of the church community, which can at times be more fiercely competitive than Wall Street. Like the time I was offered a free vacation if I could get 100 teenagers baptized in one year. In a flash I went from working for a church to a Fortune 500 company that had an "incentives for salvations" program. I must have overlooked this perk in my employee handbook.

Because the pressures to succeed in the church world can be great, asking for assistance or being in the position of needing assistance, was for me a sign of weakness and absolute destitution. Therefore, I did whatever it took to hide my situation by initiating desperate decisions in order to avoid facing the reality that I needed help.

There is a fantastic irony in writing a book that reveals to others something that most people want to keep secret. I never considered myself to have a warped sense of humor, but I laugh nervously to myself when I think of who will read these pages. It saddens me that I only let a few of our family members and friends know about our trials, but when it's hard to breathe you often cannot seem to get out the words that convey a cry for help.

I had been raised in a middle-class home that provided middle-class experiences, which in turned formed in me a middle-class psyche. Don't get me wrong, my parents are amazing and worked hard to provide for our family. I am thankful for never knowing hunger as a child, for having a roof over my head, and I always had appropriate clothing for the early 90s at my disposal. However, just like most other middle-class kids, I tended to not have a holistic understanding of other societal classes. We were sheltered by suburbia which acts as a wall that filters out what our less fortunate neighbors have to endure. Living in the suburbs is not bad, it's just not always an accurate portrayal of the various dichotomies that exists in a community.

Those born into the middle class are constantly trying to break through to the next socioeconomic class ahead of them while desperately trying to avoid the one beneath them, as if they were in some economic caste system. It is a natural cultural default of suburbia to want to be successful. There is nothing inherently wrong with wanting to be successful, until it becomes our sole ambition compounded by our desire for financial gain. The concept of welfare was not even a relevant topic in my social circles as a child. And so as an adult standing in a health and human services building designed to help those who could not operate independently in our society was for me crossing to the proverbial "other side of the tracks."

I remember waiting for my number to be called in the small stereotypical government building where I stood with others, forming this surreal line of humanity. I remember the smells of industrial strength cleaner used on the floors the night before and stale burnt coffee. I am not sure what failure smells like, but floor cleaner and bad coffee may be it. Also, if you are a government worker reading this book, can you suggest to the government elites that a more cheery décor for your buildings may be in order? The building I was in felt like the final resting place for bad hotel art. Couple all these things with elevator music in the lobby that plays random pop tracks in acoustic form, and you have yourself a complete government-funded experience.

Though it only took a few minutes for my information to be processed in a room filled with people who were trying to hold onto hope, it seemed to take an eternity. I glanced across the room at mothers corralling their children while waiting their turn to find out whether or not they would receive services. I imagined men who were busying themselves around the small government building with thoughts of unemployment running around in their heads. I could not help but wonder what each of their stories were. How did they get here? Why am I here now?

The man behind the desk asked me a question I did not fully hear, but I was able to mutter a response as I continued to look around at my fellow welfare cohorts. I sat in quiet anger wondering how I had allowed my family to enter into this realm of needing assistance. The grand irony of it all was that I was soon to be receiving benevolence that supported the same people I thought I would be helping in my ministry. I highly doubted that the concept of "suffering well" for the gospel that I had heard from so many church-planting gurus meant that pastors should be on welfare. My family was about to silently tiptoe across a cultural threshold from which I felt there was little chance of return.

Finally, I received my card containing other people's tax dollars, which would provide groceries for my growing family. In the primitive manly roles of hunter and gatherer, I had officially failed at both. I drove home in a daze trying to trace back my steps on how I had arrived at this point in my life. I felt as if there was a bumper sticker on my car that read, "Freeloader" as I took the road of shame back to my family.

Throughout the following months I grew accustomed to the stares from people in the grocery store. Often we unconsciously stare at people or situations that cause a break in our routine of everyday meanderings. We don't think we are staring too long at the special-needs child, the man picking up cans in the parking lot, or the woman panhandling on the side of the street, but when you are one of the attractions that people are staring at, you begin to realize how often we gaze a little too long at those who are different than ourselves.

I often noticed that other store patrons watched my family at the checkout line as we pulled out the extravagantly white card that showed everyone around us that, in essence, they were the ones who were actually going to be paying for our groceries today. To add to the stereotype, we have a ton of kids. We were officially the poster family for American welfare. At first I thought I was just paranoid, but after a situation where I overheard a mother comment to her daughter about "that family" with all the kids that her tax dollars were supporting which explains why they keep having kids, I realized the paranoia was not a figment of my imagination. The funny thing is you make healthier choices when on food stamps. I was almost certain that some EBT (Electronic Banking Transaction) police would pounce on our shopping cart for buying a bag of chips instead of the latest organic super food. I never ate so healthy in all my life.

On one occasion, the lady checking us out at a local grocery metropolis asked a jarring question after I entered my pin number in the POS system, "Will this be debit, credit, or EBT?" I was able to whisper to her that the card was in fact the last option she had offered. Without any hesitation she responded, "Sorry, sir, what did you say? Are you using your food stamps or a debit card?" As the beautiful blonde Texas couple behind me awaited my response with great intrigue, I silently prayed that Jesus would usher in his triumphant return in the midst of the express checkout lane at that very moment. Jesus never came, but I did end up losing my pride somewhere between the floral department and my car.

One of the hardest blows to my soul came from my youngest son who had overheard a conversation between myself and my wife concerning our financial situation while driving to the store. When we pulled up into the parking lot, my son emptied out a few coins that he had stashed away in his pocket and handed them to my wife. He then sincerely looked at the two of us and quietly said, "Here is some money to help buy us food since we don't have enough." The proverbial nail in my coffin of financial humiliation had been hammered in by a four-year-old.

I spent countless hours each day and night trying to find work and with every cover letter I sent my hatred of being on assistance grew. I did not feel God was using this situation to mold me into a better Christian for His use, but had left me long ago in order to work on another member of the church who had shown more potential. I was holding my breath because breathing seemed too much of a luxury.

I would see posts on social media outlets from friends about witnessing someone on food stamps "wasting" their money on a certain grocery item. Others would comment about how those on welfare were just "looking for handouts" and somehow were crippling the very foundation of American society (Shame on those maniacal toddlers that need to eat!). Honestly, most of the comments or political articles people posted were off-hand and not meant to hurt anyone. I think the issue of welfare provokes people to express their frustrations with a broken system the effects of which they feel each month in their own paycheck. So in some sense, I can understand their feelings. However, each comment left a bruise on my ego. My peers were passing judgment on a whole class of people and through their societal analysis they felt empowered to make sweeping generalizations. They had no idea that one of their friends fell under their veil of disparaging comments. The shame I felt was often unbearable and every comment I read made me fearful that somehow my secret had been revealed.

The public's perception of those on welfare or some sort of government assistance is a hard one to wrestle with. On the one hand many people abuse our national assistance programs and seek out every angle of exploitation. With many fast-food restaurants now accepting EBT, it becomes even easier to get frustrated with your taxes being spent on a Big Mac. On the other hand, there are those on welfare who have been left in such a difficult situation that to not assist them would violate every ethical impulse in our collective conscience. Once you are initiated into the welfare community you realize that those who really need assistance outnumber those who are abusing the system.

We want so badly to obtain simplicity concerning issues that tug at our moral objectivity, but that is not how life works. So when we cannot achieve simple answers concerning complex realities, we begin to fabricate truth while creating scenarios in our minds that lead to the creation of stereotypes. It is easier to describe every welfare participant as "lazy" instead of investigating how the individual ended up needing assistance in the first place. To be able to explain subjective situations makes us confident with feelings that sometimes do not reflect the feelings that Christ would want us to have. However, being able to explain these situations somehow feeds our lack of confidence in ourselves and allows us to create order in how we see the world.

The bottom line is that there are people who see welfare participants as a drain on our society because they assume those on welfare are gaining something for nothing. We see someone using their EBT card at the grocery store and we immediately envision all the things they could be doing to help their own situation. When we actually meet someone who is in fact taking advantage of the system we then assume everyone on welfare must be exploiting this benevolent process.

However, we often do not see Steve, the pastor I met who had to go on welfare because his church fired him over a lack of membership growth. Then there is Mark, who is on food stamps because his full-time job of caring for special needs adults pays little in currency, although he would argue the perks are amazing. Welfare is not a "one size fits all" issue and we can argue that there are very few aspects of life that truly are. People on welfare are not getting something for nothing because often the price they usually pay is in the loss of pride and hope.

When I was fresh out of college I listened to the talk radio shows, followed politicians who promoted my value system, and looked with disdain upon those who were "abusing" my tax dollars. All of these feelings were cultivated while professing to be a believer in Christ. When I was a child I saw my parents constantly pouring themselves out for other people as Jesus did for those He encountered. However, after I left the nest I saw fewer people like my parents and encountered more "modern" believers who poured out more criticism than support or love.

In my twenties I felt the average American Christian typically complained about government control, adorned morality, voted Republican, and showed off their spiritual maturity by how beat up their Bible appeared to be. I also knew that we (Christians) were to give to those in need because somewhere in the Bible God said so. However, every time I would give of my time or resources, a sense of elitism washed over me because I was the one giving benevolence and not receiving it. I did not despise the people that my church or family was helping, but I did feel slightly superior to them. In my mind I was the Good Samaritan who was straying long enough from my path of righteousness to help those in need and earning some strange merit badge of accomplishment for Team Jesus. These attitudes still bring me to repentance even as I pen these words of lament.

One of the most profound revelations while in this season of being on welfare came to me while teaching the one class that I had been able to retain. It was a simple, anticlimactic moment, but it struck such a deep chord within my heart. On a very unimportant day in the middle of one of my semesters, I arrived at class early and by chance listened in on a conversation between a few of my students as they filed into the lecture hall. A group of around five students were passionately flinging reckless comments concerning the mob in front of the welfare office down the street. Of course when I heard the word "welfare" I began to listen more closely and wondered if they had discovered my secret.

Phrases such as "They need to get a job" and "These people are so worthless" echoed off the walls of the lecture hall. There was also a racial element in these comments that was quite unsettling, but which somehow flowed so easily from these students' lips. I was shocked by their feelings, especially because many of them professed to be regenerated believers. There was something disturbing about standing in an institution built to present ideas for the sake of knowledge and instead watch it turned into a forum of judgment. Hearing my students condemning strangers was unbearable, partly because I was on welfare and mostly because I wondered if I would have in the past chimed right in with them in agreement.

Part of me wanted to interrupt my students by slinging down my EBT card on the desk like some righteous gauntlet and challenging them to a battle of social justice stump speeches. However, I sat in silence as I listened to reckless opinions that had not been filtered by life experiences. Instead of anger coming over me, I felt ashamed because I knew that I had once felt similar things about people on welfare. It was like listening to a recording of ignorance with my voice as the narrator. What had happened? How could I have fostered such feelings? How could I have drifted so far in my care for humanity? At that moment, while still silently listening to my students, I began to feel the weight of welfare lift and the winds of revelation fill my spirit.

Several more of these epiphanies would pop up from time to time while my family was on welfare which helped me realize the great disconnect that was occurring within my own heart toward those who were in need. God began to help me understand the reason I was on welfare. His plan for my family's life started to become clearer. It took me actually being on assistance to fully understand the complexities and contradictions of people who love Jesus, yet often refuse to love others because it may not seem to be in their best interest. In Scripture we never hear Christ saying, "Come to me all who are weary...as long as you are not looking for a handout," or Paul stating, "Remember the poor...if they deserve it." I realized that it was not just financial assistance I needed, but a spiritual awakening that can only come from the assistance the gospel offers to those who believe.

Often one my students each semester will ask me how they can know God at a more intimate level. This is a worthy pursuit and one that can produce overwhelming joy. However, when we ask that question, we are often met with a complex answer that goes beyond just "Read our Bibles more." Studying Scripture is a fantastic way to be introduced to the attributes and nature of God, but what about experiencing those attributes through application? I know acting upon what we learn from Scripture is considered Discipleship 101, but if it is such a basic practice, why do I feel the need to remind myself so often to exercise this basic discipline?

Jeremiah 22:16 states, "He judged the cause of the poor and needy; then it was well. Is not this to know me? declares the Lord." Jeremiah was given instructions to speak to the corrupt king of Judah who would be judging matters involving God's people. Jeremiah pleaded with the king to uphold righteousness, do what was just, and deliver those who are oppressed. In this, the king would know God and understand His nature. To know God is not to just have heard of Him or to only associate with God-fearing people. The type of life-altering knowledge of God that grows us is knowledge that pushes us to live a righteous life and influence our actions. When we are consumed with who God is and what He cares about, we should then feel the urge to take appropriate action that will reflect His concerns. While on welfare, I was able to play the part of the poor and hang around with the needy. Then and only then did I come to understand that our faith cannot be bound by knowledge accumulation alone, but that there had to be actions that were birthed from the changing of our hearts through faith in Christ.

For so many years I had given lip service to serving "the least of these," but had failed to actually act on those proclamations. When we only point to God's desire for His people to serve others, but do not actually do anything to fulfill these commands, we are not only depriving those in need of assistance, but also depriving ourselves from knowing God on a more intimate level. 1 John 3:17-18 claims, "But if anyone has the world's goods and sees his brother in need, yet closes his heart against him, how does God's love abide in him? Little children, let us not love in word or talk but in deed and in truth." Talking about serving others is cheap, but according to John, not actually serving others when we have the ability to do so is very expensive. James refers to this as being "doers" of the Word, not just "hearers" (James 1:22). In other words, stop pretending to be righteous in your cold, dead religion. Oddly, it took one of the lowest points in my life to realize that it was time to stop deceiving myself by just hearing what Jesus was asking of me, and to start making my faith tangible so that the welfare of others may be changed.

While being on welfare it became apparent that God loves me through Christ completely and that in that love is found freedom due to the actions of a forgiving Savior who sought my welfare when I needed it most. This may seem like a simple reality to the long-time believer, but this simplistic message becomes white noise to the rest of the world when we proclaim to follow a loving God yet refuse to love His Creation. I came to realize that God, through Christ, sought my welfare while I was impoverished by sin. Through His actions I was able to receive the riches of forgiveness and the wealth of restoration. In the end, after finding everything I need in Christ, I am freed to seek the welfare of other people. My actions of serving others should not be produced through grudging submission, but rather come as a response to experiencing the gospel.

There is a battle raging within us due to the residual brokenness in our makeup. Sin has marred the painting and disrupted the melody that God designed, but just like any masterpiece, we are far from done. There is still more to refine, chip away, build upon, and erase before we are completely displayed for His glory. Our hearts yearn to know more about God for we are made in His image (Genesis 1:16). However, we cannot fully know God by sitting on the sidelines with our faith in our hands, refusing to help better the welfare of other people

In the midst of being on welfare I found grace that can only come from a God with an abundance that He divvies out to the least worthy of candidates. I found the wind in my soul again. I eventually was able to breathe once more. Though money issues would often try to suffocate my family, it was obvious God was removing the weight of our material idols that had so dragged us through the muck of consumerism before we could see His mercies.

At this point in the story one usually points to a sage or wise guide who helped them "see the light." However, the wisest and most loving people in my life had no idea what I was going through. Even in my silence God allowed my heart to soften in the midst of a miserable season. With each swipe of our EBT card I felt His grace. With every form I had to fill out He opened my heart towards the plights of others. With every conversation I had to have with my children of why we could not go out to a restaurant or why we had to make homemade Christmas gifts, my value in Jesus alone became more tangible. God stripped away my pride, my security, and my defenses so that I could have nothing left but Him.

To those who venture further into this confession, let me give you some brief insight as you process the next few chapters. This book is not a step-by-step guide of how to attain some strange form of "poverty theology"; nor is it meant to hurl a guilt trip upon those who do not often help "the least of these." Our story is not nearly as hard compared to others who've been destitute and it is likely that many who read these pages have gone or will go through much more difficult trials. This book is not riddled with footnotes that would satisfy most academics; nor is it an attempt to malign a majority of Christians. It is simply a confession by someone who had to walk on the other side of the poverty line in order to understand the need for a faith that is concerned for the welfare of others because we have encountered a God who was concerned with our welfare.

Some of you may be gasping for breath because your current circumstances are sucking the air from your spirit. I will remind you of the words of Job who knew all too well what it meant to lose your breath in the face of trials. "The Spirit of God has made me, and the breath of the Almighty gives me life" (Job 33:4). Take it in. Breathe. For you are not alone and grace is not so distant that it cannot give you back your wind.

CHAPTER 2

Adventures in Dumpster Diving

One of my favorite urban sports is "dumpster diving." It is an activity that few engage in, but the rewards can be beneficial to the average suburban wanderer who desires an adventure in hipster activities. You shouldn't be too surprised about this revelation. It would seem dumpster diving should be the obvious follow-up confession to revealing that my family was on government assistance. The impoverished workers of the Lord turned to dumpster diving as a cheap alternative to grocery shopping! Sounds almost poetic.

Diving into dumpsters has become an addiction and I feel like an antiestablishment treasure hunter every time I venture out to the urban landscape. There is nothing like rummaging through the mounds of perfectly good food that our highly consumer-driven society deems unworthy of their pallet to help you play to the inner rebel inside all of us. To my fellow diving brethren out there, may your dumpsters never be locked and your produce never too ripe!

My wife and I have on occasion when entertaining friends at our house begun to engage in those funny conversations couples have that create moments of connection. There have been a few times that my wife and I feel comfortable enough to admit to our new friends that we are dumpster divers. It is a weird icebreaker or "getting to know you" practice and it often feels like we are on a bad reality show where there are hidden cameras ready to capture the unsuspecting "victim's" response.

Our friends' reactions vary, but more often than not they seemed to think it is an awesome endeavor once we explain why we dumpster dive. They typically show intrigue instead of disgust and on some occasions ask if they can come along the next time we decide to pursue trash bins for substance. I often wonder, however, at what point in the car ride back to their house they ask the question, "Did we just eat dumpster food for dinner?" I assure you we do not serve guests dumpster food the first night that we break bread with them, but the second time... all deals are off.

In Portland dumpster diving is a heralded pastime. You can find regional clubs that get together to go on eatable scavenger hunts. This odd tribe of trash collectors even has their own code of ethics such as: leave the dumpster cleaner than when you found it, take only what you need, and try not to trespass. Dumpster divers have even coined unique adjectives like "freegan," which denotes a sector of people who desire to live in a way that causes the least financial expenditures, which typically means rummaging through the excess of others. This is probably not the norm where you are from, but remember, our fair city also holds the annual naked bike ride. Dumpster diving is just another notch in our sub-cultural belt.

After listening to logical propaganda on why you should dumpster dive there is a good chance you still may not be persuaded to throw on some galoshes, grab some scuba gear, and start dumpster diving behind your local mega mart. It is not for everyone. However, being introduced to the concept of dumpster diving probably compels you to at least ask, "Why would someone do this?" Great question. In the US we will throw away 96 billion pounds of food this year alone. The Department of Agriculture claims that if the US reclaimed 5% of food that is wasted, four million people a day could be fed. Currently in the US we reclaim less than 2.5% of the food we dispose of. Finally, over half the food that is prepared in the US will be thrown out this year.[4] You may not go dumpster diving, but these sobering statistics give you a brief glimpse into food waste and cause you to pause the next time you throw out that freezer burned leftover.

One night while on a midnight dive I came across the quintessential eye-opening experience that solidified my duty to dive where no middle-class person has dived before. Just in case you are worried about the ethics of this nocturnal activity I never go to stores where there are "no trespassing" signs displayed and I would never put garbage in dumpsters, only

---

[4] Jeremy Siefert, *Dive!*, Documentary, Jeremy Siefert, (2010, Compeller Pictures, 2011.), DVD.

take "garbage" out. On many occasions I have been stopped by a police officer, store manager, or passerby, and not once have I been scolded, arrested, or made to leave. Although my encounters with non-dumpster folk usually lead them to believe I am crazy, I have never found trouble. One store manager deemed me a pioneer in food recovery. And here I thought I was just hungry.

This particular night I was about to start the evening off with a "splash" in my favorite bin where I had previously found some amazing tomatoes, tons of eggs, and even a croc pot. That may sound disgusting, but think of me as some sort of marginalized superhero rummaging through the underbelly of society in order to rescue helpless food that needed a good home. Does that help?

Patiently I waited until the last employee drove away from the store I was patrolling. To my surprise a delivery truck showed up immediately following the employee's departure. I continued to wait in my car so that my unforeseen visitor could finish his delivery and my adventure could once more resume. However, I was unable to concentrate on my strategy (which usually consisted of how to avoid getting trapped in a dumpster) due to a peculiar oddity about this delivery truck. The driver spent less time bringing in boxes to the store's warehouse and more time throwing boxes into the dumpster. After 10 minutes of seeing him fill the dumpster to the brim with unopened boxes of what I surmised was food, I had to get out and ask what he was doing.

The first few minutes of the conversation had that tone of awkwardness that one may expect at midnight behind a grocery store. The deliveryman just started at me as I explained the nature of my business. His first question to me after I told him of my journey in farming dumpsters was, "Does your wife know you are out here?" After I assured him she did (which seemed to vex him further) I asked what was in all these boxes that he had tossed into the dumpster. "Chicken," he explained, "frozen chicken to be exact." According to the driver this abundance of frozen chicken was supposed to be delivered to another store several hours away, but accidentally got placed on his truck. He noted that it was cheaper due to fuel and labor costs to reorder the food than to drive a few hours to the correct store. As well, there was a lack of storage at the location where we were having this conversation.

I was dumbfounded. This dumpster food was not the normal bounty that I would typically find. Most of the time a dumpster diver will discover food that is still eatable, just not as "pretty" as the consumer would like. Items such as: produce that by morning would start to look a little shabby in the store's display stands, cartons of eggs thrown out because one egg had cracked during delivery, dented cans that had fallen from the shelves, or the occasional meat (which is rare...) whose "best sold on" date had come and gone.

The food I found often had not been in the dumpster for more than an hour and would be perfectly good food even to a non-dumpster diver's standards. However, these boxes did not contain the typical dumpster food I was accustomed to, but actually had perfectly normal food, fresh from the distributor, that would have been displayed the next day for any shopper who uses the normal way of grocery shopping to purchase. I was ecstatic to find such a haul, yet saddened at the absolute tragedy occurring before my own eyes.

The driver allowed me to grab as many boxes as I wanted as he finished unloading his truck. All in all I took home seven boxes of frozen chicken that each had around 15 pieces of chicken in each unit. We gave most of it away, but we did eat chicken for quite some time.

Two things happened that night other than hitting the food gold mine. The first was that regardless the number of people who go hungry in the US, we still find ways to be extravagant in the way we waste our resources. The second was changing one's perspective, no matter how great or small, is sometimes best gained through unforeseen experiences. I drove back to my house that night with the windows down and the radio off so I could process what had just happened. What some would see as a random event that involved frozen chicken, I saw as a deeply troubling scenario of waste that led me to wonder if I was contributing to this problem by throwing away the tangible and spiritual resources God had delivered to me?

Perspective is shaped by a series of enlightening encounters that allow us to see both sides of the proverbial coin in order to gain wisdom, insight, and often direction. When I first heard about dumpster diving my middle-class instincts kicked in and I could not fathom why people would stoop to such a stunt. All I could imagine was a rotting food paradise where rats went on vacation to get away from the day-to-day grind of rodent life. However, it was not until I actually attempted dumpster diving, educated myself on how food actually is preserved, and experience first-hand the massive amount of wasteful consumerism that happens every week at our grocery stores, that I gained perspective.

Perspective is a powerful tool that can change a person's core, altering beliefs and emotions that were once so deeply rooted in one's DNA. It could be argued that a fresh perspective (allowed by God) is one of the human catalysts that have inspired historic charitable movements. Unsuspecting persons gain perspective through an unplanned experience thus compelling them to create change so that others may avoid similar experiences.

Prior to going on assistance I had misplaced feelings for people who were on welfare before "perspective" was forced upon me through financial loss. It was not until I got a small taste of life below the poverty line that I began to finally understand not just what people on welfare were feeling, but that I was also complicit in the societal judgment they encountered every day. Due to circumstances that I had not expected, an unforeseen perspective was thrust upon me that caused me to want to change myself as well as have a positive effect on others.

When I was in elementary school we had a free lunch program similar to what we have today. I remember standing in line waiting for what the cafeteria was trying to pass off as nutrition when I realized my friend Mark, who was standing in front of me, forgot to pay the cashier for his food. He simply told the woman his name and was able then to proceed to the dining area. I sat down next to Mark after purchasing my food and asked him why he did not have to pay. He began to explain to me the government lunch program as best as one fourth-grader could explain it to his peer. What a great deal! Eat not one, but two meals for free! Mark also told me that his family paid for food with stamps. You can imagine my grade-school bewilderment. I heard of stamp collectors, but I did not realize you could cash them in for Twinkies.

Mark and I continued to be friends up until middle school when sociological factors and divergent interests have a way of naturally separating people. It's not that I didn't want to associate with Mark anymore or felt he was unworthy of my company. Mark and I simply lived vastly different lives. Though we probably unconsciously made assumptions about what the other's life was like, we really had no idea what had driven us apart.

As I made my way through school it seemed Mark had created his own tribe of friends that ran around together just like the popular kids did--the band people, the jocks, etc. It was as if Mark's friends understood the hardships each other was enduring and shared a perspective on what the other was going through. So naturally they clung to one another. When groups, non-profits, or social justice organizations form it is typically based on key foundational beliefs that everyone in the group comprehends and champions. Powerful community can manifest itself in shared experiences and passions that can provoke both positive and negative change. Mark wanted to be around people that understood him, share his perspective, and who had similar experiences. Whether it was intentional or not, we will cling to people that have similar perspectives as ours and build walls to keep those with different perspectives out. We stop communicating and just make assumptions, which in the end damages our effectiveness in making positive changes.

I think it was this idea of understanding another's plight that made signing up for welfare so difficult for me. I thought I was very savvy concerning what people on welfare were going through and felt obliged to make judgments on them because I had been educated, I had been exposed to the stereotypes, and I had been told my entire life that I was going to succeed. I built caricatures of people in my head who exhibited certain behaviors, sins, and shortcomings. Once I had met one person who was addicted to drugs, I assumed I could transfer their story to the next addict. It is as if I had some database that contains descriptions of every debauchery I encounter so that I could make sure to place them in the correct narrow category of deviancy.

My knowledge of the welfare community expanded greatly the day I left that Health and Human Services Office. Before too long I began to meet many others that had similar stories to mine. The chasm that I had always perceived between people who were on government assistance and myself completely disintegrated after my family had to use generosity to fill our pantry. This realization caused me to ask myself what other similarities or common threads exist that connect people to one another regardless of their backgrounds. Then it became clear that there is a common trait that all mankind has maintained since the first person ever walked the earth: Anyone who has ever taken a breath has at times used some of them to sin.

No matter what our stock portfolio or bank account shows, we are all impoverished people. Monetary poverty is only one type of hardship that hits a particular portion of a population. Sin, on the other hand, has been impoverishing people since the beginning of time and none are immune to its infection.

This may seem strange coming from a pastor who had attended several lectures at a respected seminary, but it was not until I was on welfare that I fully understood the position that all of us find ourselves in when it comes to sin. My opinion of people on welfare changed which led me to understand that there were other key prejudices residing in my heart towards others who are different from me. I understand that for most this is no real grand revelation, but for me it was an epic heart shift from judgment to compassion.

Whether we are facing economic woes, struggling with addiction, or any other indulgence on the sin buffet the fact remains that if we are of the human race then we are all broken and in need of redemption. So instead of seeing the drunk, the liar, the prostitute, the liberal, the conservative, the rich, or the poor, I finally was able to see the unique human being before me whom God had crafted. I think that's how God operates. We can at times only see our failures because for us they are obvious and ever present. God on the other hand sees Jesus in us, which I have to imagine makes Him smile. It's not that He is blind to our shortcomings, but I think He sees the potential of what Christ can do in us and understands that we are more than the sum of our mistakes. We are more, because He has made us more.

This impoverished sinful state comes solely from our own doing and we are unable to fix our situation without outside assistance. Our natural tendency is to focus on the idols that draw our attention away from God, which ultimately propels us into a self-worship pattern that leaves us spiritually bankrupt. We are cast into the streets of mayhem that have been paved by fractured hearts that are searching for manmade answers that only lead to another empty road. Many of us will search for temporary relief through morality, pragmatism, or religious ramblings; yet without Jesus these manmade solutions are simply fixes from a needle that contains the intoxicating drug of self-righteousness and leaves us with a false security. We are the architects of our spiritually impoverished state, which in a beautiful way puts us all on equal footing when it comes to who to blame for our separation from a righteous God.

On the first day of each semester in the college classes I teach, every one of my students has an equal chance of gaining the highest level of achievement. There have been no tests, quizzes, term papers, or projects completed to act as judge and jury of any student's aptitude. On the first day everyone is Einstein, the smartest kid in the class, until that faithful day when the first assessment is completed. By the time final exams come around my small community of students has been divided according to letter grade. Each of them is diligently trying to either maintain their standing or try to achieve a better grade that would increase their sense of well-being.

Unlike the classroom that will routinely separate the astute and the not-so-astute, sin acts as the great equalizer that has no regard for performance, knowledge, and ability. It is a virus that infects the wise and the foolish alike. Since we are all crippled with sin then all of us need a solution.

Every human being is in the same welfare boat when it comes to sin. It would sink were it not for some outside Helper to come and take us to the shores of peace. Sin levels the playing field and throws our judgmental attitudes into oblivion. It makes all of us keenly aware that we are just as capable of any action or decision made by any other person that we will encounter.

Sin has caused us to accumulate an irrefutable case of guilt. The chances of us reversing our well-deserved sentence of separation from God would be insurmountable. There is absolutely nothing within our own power that could relieve us from the sin that has stained our soul; there are no pragmatic steps we can take to change our situation.[5] There is no amount of penance or good deeds that can expunge our record of misconduct. This very reality is why Christ was promised by

---

[5] Paul makes it clear in Galatians 2:21 that if we were masters of our own righteousness, then Christ's death would be pointless and one could even come to the conclusion that His sacrifice is almost cruel.

God to be His missionary to Creation in order to reverse our fate.[6]

In many religions across the globe the individual faith pursuer believes that they must modify their behavior so as to attain a higher level of morality if they hope to be in union or in touch with their god(s). Yet when we pause for a moment and think upon who we really are, not the person that everyone perceives you to be in public, but the type of person you are when no one is watching. When we reflect on our shortcomings, we must ask ourselves, "how good do I have to be to accepted by god?" Many toil in their daily lives trying to appease a deity or even people so that they can be accepted, but how good do our efforts need to be in order to overcome our sin? Can we be good enough to be accepted by a righteous entity?

The beautiful truth is that our efforts could never be good enough to rectify our sinful nature. Our good works cannot overcome the debt that our rebellious hearts have acquired, and our deeds do not move us to the forefront of God's pleasure.[7] Thankfully, instead of us having to aim for higher moral platitudes to try to impress God, He saw our absolute inability to achieve reconciliation through our individual efforts—and came to us. We were impoverished due

---

[6] Ephesians 2:1-9 speaks to this idea of God sending Christ because of his grace and mercy, not due to our worthiness. The gift of financial assistance contains imagery that reminds of the gift of salvation that God has granted those of us in need.

[7] Romans 3:28

to sin and He gave us His assistance, for the sake of our welfare and for His glory.

Romans 5:8 states, "But God shows his love for us in that while we were still sinners, Christ died for us." This is a familiar passage to most believers and one that is critical to cultivating a heart that seeks the welfare of others. Our sin nature separates us from achieving community with God. Since not one person is exempt from needing this assistance, we can lay aside our prejudice and see the welfare participant, the lawyer, the addict, and the CEO as all needing Christ. Our "success" in being a good person does not move us closer to God, but our admittance that we can't be good enough to be in relationship with God is the first step to understanding how His economic system works. We don't clean ourselves up through good deeds so God will love us, we are loved by God so that we are freed to do good works.

The assistance we needed as finite and flawed humans came from an infinite God whose forgiveness affords us a relationship with Him and each other. 1 John 4:19 claims, "We love for He first loved us." This passage is inscribed on my wedding band due to the absolute passion my wife has for Christ. For many years it was for me simply a verse that Christians use at momentous occasions. And then I came to realize that we cannot fathom what real love is until God first loves us through Christ. Love is merely a chemical reaction of the endorphins in our brain cells. It is only Christ who empowers us to understand the bottomless depths of true sacrificial love. This type of love is achieved solely by God creating, initiating, and displaying this love to us and in us.

When we hold onto the gospel whereby God is the author of our redemption, only then do I think that we are able to see people as He sees them. A God-initiated gospel awakens our minds to the idea of grace, which empowers our hearts to show grace towards others. The social circles we hide in begin to unravel and we allow ourselves to be exposed to varying perspectives.

The problem is that we want control our lives and our righteousness. We practice moral behaviors, work diligently to be "successful," and brag about our achievements, all so that society will say that we have chosen the righteous path and that others should take a lesson from our moral playbook. The ramification of holding such beliefs spills over to our salvation. At one point I truly felt it was solely because of my choices, my decisions, my righteous thinking, and my moral compass that I had achieved a right standing with God, when in fact, it was all due to a loving God who had sought me in my helpless condition and had redeemed my welfare state through the sacrificial gift of His Son.

So what does this have to do with dumpster diving and people on welfare? If you were to just causally hear about dumpster diving you more than likely would make an instant (and probably negative) judgment over such an activity. Just as if you saw a man standing beside a busy highway asking for spare change, you may in an instant presume to know how he came to be there. Yet if you were to brave diving into a dumpster or dive into relationships with the marginalized, then your perspective may well change, causing your thoughts and actions to follow suit.

I still to this day do not fully comprehend why God allowed my family to be on welfare, but I do know that from the experience I learned little about fiscal responsibility that I did not already know. What I did gain was a new perspective that will forever be the lens through I can rightly view my neighbors. Regardless of circumstances or societal statuses, we are in this together. Our souls are poverty-stricken because of sin, and we all need outside assistance.

I still dumpster dive on occasion though there is no longer a need. I suppose I do so because it is truly a treasure hunt and serves as a decent midlife-crisis activity. I also continue to do it as a way to remind myself of the perspective I achieved that allowed me to look past the exterior that each individual displays for all the world to see and realize that we are all on the same journey. All of us, no matter their ethnicity, backstory, or economic prowess, are on the inside vagabonds in need of a redemption that can only be found through Jesus. Perspective can be a wonderful thing, especially when it allows us to see with the eyes of Jesus who gave His all so that we might see others not for just who they are, but who they could be.

CHAPTER 3

Safety In Numbers

I met my wife at a coffee shop and awkwardly used a Christian pickup line to get her attention. There are typical pickup lines and then there are Christian pickup lines which are much more painful to hear out loud. I think Jesus Himself looked away in embarrassment when I first tried to introduce myself to my future bride. She wisely found a way to quickly get out of the conversation and excused herself to the bathroom in order to escape from the creeper with no fashion sense. Eventually, I wore her down and convinced her to go on a date with me. She has never let me live down my terrible attempt to hit on her.

My wife makes me feel safe. I would argue that feeling safe is one of the greatest emotions we can experience. Not the type of safety that comes from wearing a seatbelt or bike helmet, but the safety that comes from knowing someone almost as well as you know yourself. Happiness can fade, excitement never endures, optimism can be fleeting, but true safety guaranteed by a loving God seems to be able to withstand the harshness of time. When I am around my wife the sirens of this world are quieted and anxiety cannot find a foothold in my soul. This type of security can only be achieved when someone knows precisely how you are wired. To be known is to achieve freedom because there is someone out there who has accepted you at your best and not tossed you aside when you are at your worst.

Having a faith that is concerned for the welfare of others shares similar elements to that of a marriage relationship. In order for someone to ask for help they need to feel safe. In order for them to feel safe, they need to be known. However, it is scary to be known because then we begin to confront how messy people are and how messy our own life can be. Despite the difficulty of being vulnerable in a relationship, there is nothing like transparency that initiates the first step of healing. The result of combining security and relational transparency will often lead to healthy community.

Right now it seems all of Christendom is trying to put their arms around what it means to have "community." This is a worthy pursuit for the art of relationship is one of the key foundations to the Christian faith. At every waypoint of our faith we have a relational element. We are brought into a relationship with God. We are ushered into a relationship with the church and we seek to build relationships with other people in order that they may join us in community with God. Christianity is a cyclical faith, always reproducing itself through the bonds that form between people and God.

I hesitate to define "community" because the idea of community is a constantly evolving human experience. However, one brief element of community, defined in the loosest of terms, could be seen as the cultivating of positive and frequent connections with another person or people to the point where bonds of familiarity, investment, and safety are formed. My wife and I share an element of community in our marriage. I am connected with her more intimately than any other person on this earth and we have had shared experiences that have defined our story. We have had positive experiences, wonderful adventures, pushed through conflict, and we are constantly connecting at various levels. All of our connections and feelings of safety have been forged first by our connection with Christ. Knowing Jesus has allowed us as a couple to endure welfare, the loss of two children via miscarriage, and discovering that my oldest son Noah has autism.

When my wife and I received Noah's official diagnosis I found myself immediately in a fog. I had read about other parents going through these situations with their children, but you never expect to be living out one of those stories. I was so wrapped up into how this affected me that I had forgotten about my wife and Noah altogether. I retreated into isolation and did not want to talk about the unique challenges my son was going to face. I began to walk in denial that this was actually happening to my son and denial quickly led to blaming myself for something that I had no hand in.

In the beginning, my wife Cassie dealt with everything having to do with Noah. His treatment, therapy, medication, and paperwork were thrust upon her shoulders because I simply could not comprehend what was happening. It took some time for me to finally accept that Noah had autism and that our lives were just going to look different from here on out. My wife was truly an amazing hero during this time. I watched as she approached Noah as the wonderfully unique son who was going to take the world's breath away.

I remember watching my wife for hours get on the floor to help him regain his motor skills and have endless conversations with him knowing a response would more than likely not come. My wife did not see a barricade to happiness, but instead just a hurdle that needed to be conquered. My wife made our son feel safe, and as a family we began to have experiences that we never expected. After six months I repented to my wife for my distance and began to accept the story that God was writing for our family. I rejoined normal life and sought out community with a new sense of assurance.

At 18 months, Noah had lost all of his language and most of his motor skills. We were told by a child psychologists that we should prepare ourselves for Noah never to speak and he would more than likely never be independent. There is not a parenting class or technique that can prepare you for those types of conversations. I remember Noah standing in the corner playing with some toys while the psychologist was explaining to us his new reality. Noah showed no interest at all in what was being said and would just look at us from time to time to make sure we were still around. It felt unnerving to be discussing the possible limitations of my first-born in his presence, yet he never seemed to pay much attention to the adults in the room who were planning out his future.

Right after Noah's third birthday, he decided to reintroduce himself officially to his family and the world. I remember making pancakes for our crew when Noah walked into the kitchen and just stared at me as I went through our morning routine. I began to talk to him about the day's activities and then ended our morning conversation asking him what type of drink he wanted to pair with his breakfast, although I did not expect a response. Then Noah did something that will be etched in my mind forever. He casually walked over to the refrigerator, pointed, and exclaimed, "Orange juice, please." I stared at him just as intently as he had been previously staring at me. His small little voice sounded to me like a grand orchestra filling an ornate hall with the sound of melodious notes. Of course I did what any father would do: I yelled with such excitement for my wife to come into the kitchen that she thought the house was on fire.

Noah had about two gallons of orange juice that day because he kept repeating the same phrase and we kept rewarding him with what he was asking for. God's mercy was thick that morning and though I would be just as happy if Noah had never spoke, God's loosening his tongue was one of many unwarranted gifts that He has blessed us with through this precious boy. It seemed Noah had decided it was time to be heard and to this day he still loves his orange juice.

"Noah the Conqueror" is now an amazing brother to six other siblings. He is their hero and the leader of our offspring.

He inspires me to want more out of life and to love unconditionally as he does. Noah is such an amazing example of God's workmanship. With each passing year more and more people are impacted by my son. Noah has a way of breaking through social barriers that many of us will never conquer. Whereas I feel slightly awkward trying to meet someone for the first time, Noah does not see a stranger, but a new friend. I have never seen a child who desires community as passionately as Noah. Wherever he goes, happy people follow.

Community involves familiarity, comfort, security, and passion. It's the desire not to sit in the darkness of trials, but to come into the light of confession as others are allowed into your situation. There are so many people living amongst us who are alone, aching for someone to care about them. However, we often do not approach people like Noah does, not seeing the external appearance of people, but who instead with his ten-year-old eyes sees their essence. People are not just empty beings passing to and fro for his amusement, judgment, or entertainment. Everyone, regardless of their appearance or mannerisms, has value to Noah and is worthy of being engaged.

Parents of a special-needs child typically run into the same people all the time. It's as if your kid is on a traveling sports team and all the parents find themselves at the same events so naturally you befriend a few of them after several encounters. If you get into a room of parents of special-needs kids you will hear a whole other language being spoken that's made up of mostly medical terms that seems to emulate a modern-day Babble.

Within these circles you find you have shared experiences, similar struggles, and familiar hopes. Natural community is cultivated and you cheer for the welfare of one another. When a special-needs child of another parent experiences victories, in a strange way you feel victorious to, while their setbacks grieve you way beyond the point of empathy. You know that you are all on the same journey, and although no one can explain how exactly you got there, all you know is that it feels better to have passengers along for the ride.

Community is a fickle thing, especially in the midst of complicated struggles. When I see a child with large headphones on that would rival those seen in hip hop videos circa 1993 or a child meticulously lining up trains in the toy aisle at the store, I instantly feel a connection with them and their parents. It makes me want to seek the parents out, introduce myself, give hugs to total strangers while telling them it is going to be alright, and to defend them from onlookers who do not understand.

We are made to desire, seek out, and be a part of community because of the image of the One who made us. God designed us to need and depend on one another. When He created man in His image, He did so as God the Father, God the Son, and God the Spirit.[8] God has always been in perfect community with Himself, so being His image-bearers and sharing in His attributes, we should sense a longing to be in close relationship with one another. It is in community we exercise how God desires us to function. Remember the last

---

[8] Genesis 1:26

time you stayed up late with a group of friends, enjoyed good food, and engaged in deep conversations? Ideas, fears, hopes, dreams, opinions, and affirmations were flung about wildly the entire night and when the evening had come to an end, an ever so slight feeling of mourning crept in your heart. I believe that is God, revealing to you that life is simply better when we are together with others that care for us as much as we care for them.

Through these intimate relationships we are then united through a common bond to seek the welfare of others and allow others to concern themselves with our welfare. Paul urges us Galatians 6:2 to "bear one another's burdens" in order to emulate Christ. Our newfound life in Jesus gives us freedom to take on the burdens of others with joyful hearts in gratitude for the burden of sin that was lifted from us through Christ. A self-sacrificing mindset overtakes us and joy fills our being when we help others solely in response to Christ helping us.

I remember sitting in a support group for parents with special-needs children and watching as a couple confessed their deep isolation due to their low-functioning autistic son. They wept in front of total strangers and bared their grief before a sympathetic audience. Afterwards I approached them and asked if I could pray for them, as well as have their entire family over to our house for dinner. The father was the first to quickly reject my offer, explaining that they cannot engage in such social activities because their son may cause a scene, break something, or become aggressive. No matter how much I pleaded with them he still refused. Finally, the husband was frustrated enough with my insistent behavior he asked me pointblank how I could be so positive despite my own son's condition. Before I could answer, he then asked a second question that has since replayed in my mind countless times, "Do you think your son will actually be fixed one day?"

"Fixed." I am not even sure what that means. My mind raced as I asked myself, "How do you fix the love that pours from Noah's eyes when he engages with his siblings? How do you fix the honest emotions that come from Noah when he is ecstatic or downtrodden? How do you fix the joy that comes from the depths of his heart when he meets a new friend and cannot stop talking about them for months on end? How do you fix his inquisitive response to stimuli that seems common to everyone else?" Though my mind was racing, I calmly responded with the first thing that popped up into my mind: "My son cannot be fixed, because he is not broken."

The tone of my answer was not one of judgment, but rather from a father who had carried the same weight for a season as these two people were now hauling around. I then began to explain to them that Noah was wonderfully made and that out of all the parents in the world, God chose to honor my wife and me to be his caregivers. The husband was not content with my answer and retorted from a hurting heart, "Why would God ever allow this type of thing?"

Why is there hurting in the world? Why do bad things happen? Why is this happening to us? These were some of the many questions that were hiding behind his initial question. I responded in the only way I knew how: "I don't know...but I do know that someday it will all make sense." I could have gone into a lecture about how sin has broken Creation and how there are consequences due to this brokenness, but this father did not need a sermon; he just needed to feel safe enough to vent his frustrations.

Oddly, even in this tense moment, we were sharing a version of community even though it may not have seemed like a positive experience. Community is not always laughter and joy; it can also produce pain and grief. However, if someone feels safe and vulnerable during times of community, the tone of the exchange, although intense, can lead to healthy outcomes. It is in these moments we can allow our pain to come to the surface so that others are aware of the struggles we are carrying within ourselves.

The couple never again came back to the support group and I never was able to reconnect with this hurting family. I want to think that they found community. I hope that wherever life took them they and their son are at peace. I often think of them when I meet other parents of special-needs children and I wonder if the husband ever found the answers to his daunting questions.

All too often these types of situations end with people silently struggling to improve their welfare without any semblance of support. The act of asking for help is a difficult one to initiate, yet the need for assistance from outside sources is a foundational element prescribed within the human experience. We often project ourselves as creatures who thrive in this "lone ranger" approach to life, but in the midst of these pursuits we often forget that God is weaving lives together in a grand support network forged by His glory.

There were many days while we were on welfare that I wondered why God had placed us in such a demoralizing position. We could not afford my son's therapy, even though we knew he needed it. I knew God understood our situation, but to be honest I often wondered why He was not making the adjustments to our life that we so desperately needed. Where was our "breakout" moment when everything would fall into place? I realize now that God was taking us through this season of hardship to reveal more of Himself to us, but during that time it was difficult to see a reason behind our lack of finances. No matter how much I pondered why our family was on food stamps, it never occurred to me to confide in another human being for comfort and wisdom.

The subject of welfare was at the time for me a taboo topic. The truly sad part about feeling this way is that I met weekly with two close friends for accountability who loved Jesus and me. I constantly confessed to these men my failures as a friend, husband, and father, and yet admitting we were struggling financially and that I was agonizing over the fact that I was on government assistance seemed too heavy of a burden to lay on these dear brothers. At the same time, I was encouraging special-needs families to join in a community setting, while choosing not to prescribe the same remedy for my own family's struggle.

The fears of asking for help for our physical, emotional, and spiritual needs often translate to an unhealthy view of community. Confessing addictions, repenting of sin, and admitting shortcomings do not seem appealing at all to our individualistic nature. To ask for accountability, guidance, and wisdom is often perceived wrongly as a sign of immaturity. Out of fear of facing judgment, many will continue to combat their struggles in silence, hoping they will grow out of it or achieve peace through some manufactured plan that is based on their individual efforts to relieve them of their situation. After they fail to find relief because they've pinned their hopes on their own abilities, they become frustrated and often lose hope. Being on welfare was definitely a daunting situation that made me feel like I had washed up on a strange island of misfits. I look back now on how I might have had some answers or at least some comfort concerning our situation sooner if I had just simply sought out others for help.

Romans 8: 28 states, "And we know that for those who love God all things work together for good, for those who are called according to his purpose." This verse is on the all-time top ten list of most misused Scriptures. Many pull it out of its context in order to use it for their own purposes. I have heard this passage preached as a prescription for prosperity, an axe for zealous legalists, and a crutch for those who waiver in their faith. To understand Romans 8:28, you have to understand the heart of what the entire chapter seeks to convey.

Romans 8:1 drives this whole passage when it states, "There is therefore no condemnation for those who are in Christ Jesus." The reality that in Jesus we are not left to the deadly demise that we so richly deserve is reason enough to rejoice. Our sin condemns us in every sector of our being, yet shrouded in the grace of Christ we have life (8:11), we are adopted as the children of God (8:14), and all things have worked out for us because we were given the ability to love God through Christ (8:28). "All things" in our life are working together "for good" because there is no condemnation in Christ. Verse 28 does not point us to some prosperity road full of pragmatic steps to receive God's blessings in the form of earthly possessions or perfect health, but is instead an assurance that God is the Lord of every situation in your life and is working these moments together for His own glory which will always be good for us. If God is in control, then the relationships He has given you or desires to give you, are part of His plan of working everything out for your good and for His glory.

Hebrews 10:24-25 states, "And let us consider how to stir up one another to love and good works, not neglecting to meet together, as is the habit of some, but encouraging one another, and all the more as you see the Day drawing near." When life is going well, we want to share our happiness with others. When we feel like there is not a day that goes by in which something doesn't go wrong, we tend to want to put some distance between ourselves and others. Often this feeling of retreat is because we are either so depressed that we do not want to spread our misery to our friends or we think that no one really cares about what we are going through. On the contrary, the author of Hebrews is giving a prescription to those who are hurting. God has brought us, His children, together so that we can encourage one another, to care about each other's issues, and to cultivate or "stir up" one another to love. The only way this is possible is if we do not neglect gathering together in community. In this communal setting hope is found not in prescribing solutions for one another, but in reflecting on the gospel that points to the "Day drawing near" when as believers we will experience the return of Christ. There will be no more pain, no more weeping, and no more suffering. There will only be pure community with God and one another.

I recently took a hike with my family through Silver Falls National Park 40 minutes south of Portland. The park maintains several natural waterfalls and is one of the most serene places I have ever known. Walking literally under the South Fall is breathtaking, but on my last visit I was struck with awe by something else. As you walk the trailheads you notice an intricate pattern of giant trees that produce an amazing assortment of green leaves and pine needles that create a canopy over certain parts of the park. The tapestry of trees protects the traveler below from the rain that frequently falls in Oregon. Some rain is able to seep through this natural canopy, but most of it is caught amongst the trees, which allows for a mostly dry hike for those beneath them along the path. Though this canopy keeps out some of the rain, when the sun begins to shine it is as if the trees themselves move to the side so that the travelers can behold the beautiful light coming down from the sky.

When you seek the welfare of others through community, a similar effect occurs. The traveler is facing a possible storm on the trail that is taking them to their final destination. They see the clouds looming and even feel drops of turmoil that warn them this next portion of their hike will be contentious. However, the traveler is surrounded by a community that will help them contend with this difficult part of their journey and block out as much of their burdens as possible, while allowing the light to shine thus reminding the traveler that better days lie ahead.

Being on welfare was not an ideal social situation, but it would have been nice to have shared that struggle with a community of people whom I know loved us. From all of this I have learned that difficulties come and go, yet authentic communal relationships remain, even during the hardest of seasons. Some of you reading this may need to reach out to one of those people in your life with whom you feel safe and let them in on the fight you find yourself in the midst of. They may not solve the issue for you, but at least they can jump into the fight alongside you, applying the promises of the gospel as you struggle through this season.

I stopped long ago trying to cure Noah, because he does not need to be cured. Noah has ushered our family into so many amazing communities and conversations that I will be forever in his debt. My son continues to conquer the obstacles that autism brings while we continue to understand as a family that we are never alone, and never will be.

CHAPTER 4

Successful Humans

I have never owned a house. I would like to one day own a house, but I am 35 years old and I have never owned my own home. Closing costs, counter-offers, and inspections are terms that have never been relevant to my life thus far. Former students who were once part of my ministry are now home-owning adults. Landlords and leases I get, but being a homeowner has never been a title that I can attach to my name.

It may seem strange, but since I was young I always envisioned owning my own home. A weird ambition for a 10-year-old for sure, but I suppose it came from the fact that I lived in the same home nearly my entire childhood. My home always felt like a safe place where my needs were always met. I felt stability and consistency because I knew that I could depend on showing up to my house and finding all the essentials one needs to feel....at home. I understand now how fortunate I was to have had these amenities in my life along with parents who loved me well. So it is only natural that I would want the same thing for my kids.

There is however a more selfish, even sinful reason for my longing to own a house. For some reason I have always felt that owning a house would mean that I was successful. To be able to procure a piece of earth seems like a way to stake your claim in the world in order to announce that you are in fact are an adult and have achieved something important. For me, not owning a home has always felt like I was missing a step in my ascendance into adulthood. Some may have similar feelings towards their lack of a career, the absence of a mature relationship, or failing to achieve a certain level of education. Over the years our society has established certain benchmarks which we must evolve into so that we cannot just feel like an adult, but a successful one at that.

From the time I entered public school I was convinced that there was a particular formula I needed to adhere to in order to be successful. Go to school, get into college, earn a degree, find a job, get married, buy a house, have kids, and retire to Florida so I could complain about the weather. Simple enough. Why is it then that many people achieve these milestones, yet still feel incomplete and wonder if they had missed something along the way?

Bill was an older gentleman who attended the church I used to pastor in Portland. He was dying of lung cancer and he knew his time on this earth was almost up. I visited him at the hospital to try to comfort him in his final days on this planet. We talked for half an hour about nurses, bed sores, and treatments. Then without warning he began to tear up. He looked at me and said, "I would give it all back if I could." Not really knowing how to respond to this sudden shift in the conversation I just stared at him, waiting for him to elaborate. He then began to tell me about how many houses he had owned, businesses he had run, and all the success he had gained in his lifetime. He told me that he wished he had walked away from it all instead of letting a nasty divorce drive his wife and kids away from him for years. He wished he had more friends and fewer business associates. "All my success that I have gained," he said, "will never outweigh the amount of regret that I still hold onto."

Bill died a few weeks later and I was given the charge to preach his funeral. I was nervous wondering if anyone would show up and if they did, what their response would be to this man who had been good at accumulating success, yet, according to him, not very accomplished at accumulating relationships. I pulled into the church parking lot and to my surprise the entire lot was overflowing with cars. People were clamoring to get a seat inside the tiny sanctuary. I sat in my car absolutely stunned.

The funeral was unlike any I had ever conducted. People began to tell stories in the middle of the service (unprompted, I might add) about Bill that were hilarious and uplifting. I finally had to put a stop to all the stories or the service would have lasted through the night. Here was a man who on his deathbed was so blinded by his own "success" that he felt he had not made the slightest impact on those who were close to him. Yet here at his funeral there were 200 people who would beg to differ.

Philippians 4:19 states, "And my God will supply every need of yours according to his riches in glory in Christ Jesus." Paul was reminding the church at Philippi that everything we need will be given to us by God according to the riches He possesses in the person of Christ. According to Paul, God inundates us with spiritual riches through Jesus via the grace that comes from the gospel. What a wonderful truth to be reminded of, and yet too often our lives lead us to believe that these riches are not enough to sustain us. Like Bill we get so wrapped up in pursuing earthly comfort that often we do not realize how many people we have impacted in our lifetime.

Despite what Christ has given to us, at times there is still this feeling that we lack something or need more of something in order to be satisfied. We try to bargain with God to just allow us to be in a particular relationship, find that perfect job, or own that dream house, promising Him that then we will be satisfied with His provisions. But when the things we ask for do not arrive, then we are prone to think that God does not care about making us happy and that He may not even have a plan for our lives. We give God way too many ultimatums, demanding that He give us something more apart from Jesus or we simply won't be happy.

On the other hand, when we acquire that perfect job or meet that special someone whom we feel will finally make us complete, we find after a while that we are still not wholly satisfied. These idols of the heart are simply symptomatic of the struggle within our soul caused by constantly trying to supplant God as the center of our joy with worldly desires. The problem is that we are looking at these milestones in life to complete us, but they were never created to do that. However, we run to creation nonetheless to give us self-worth, satisfaction, and joy. When that relationship or job does not do bring those things to us, we find ourselves discarding those things to seek out "better" things that will surely make us happy. We jump on a carousel of disappointment not realizing we are just going around in circles.

When I was a kid my family attended a large Baptist church where practically every member was somehow related to me. I remember being introduced to Jeremiah 29:11 at this church and being told it was an "incentives verse" that promises us total happiness. In this verse Jeremiah reveals what God had said to him when he wrote," For I know the plans I have for you, declares the Lord, plans for welfare and not for evil, to give you a future and a hope." I think Americans love this verse more than the rest of the world does. We have it on coffee cups, framed on the walls of our homes. It's a particular favorite "go-to" verse when something good happens to us.

The next three verses state, "Then you will call upon me and come and pray to me, and I will hear you. You will seek me and find me, when you seek me with all your heart. I will be found by you, declares the Lord, and I will restore your fortunes and gather you from all the nations and all the places where I have driven you, declares the Lord, and I will bring you back to the place from which I sent you into exile." Jeremiah is giving hope to the people of Israel that God will one day redeem them and all of Creation, putting everything in its proper order. It is a prelude to the gospel of Christ in that God desires those whom He has exiled from His presence due to their sin will one day be brought back into a renewed relationship with Him.

These verses ought to be very encouraging, but they have also become the mantra for a certain sect of heretical Christianity known as the "prosperity gospel." The (mostly) well-intentioned pastors who promote this false belief system argue that God wants us to have perfect health, material wealth, and wisdom in abundance. All we need to do, they say, is to believe that God will give you these things and you will receive them if the amount of faith you put in the request is sufficient to please God. To them, God's "plans for welfare...to give you a future and a hope" means He's going to give you a big, new house along the coast. But what this "gospel" actually does is turn God's blessings into a lottery in which only the most dedicated believers will ever strike it rich. These pastors will pull verses out of context, isolate certain ones that affirms this "theology," and often experience wealth themselves due to the patrons they attract to their church looking for the "good life."

I'm not saying God does not want to provide for you. However, God does not have a standing commission that all of us should possess an excessive amount of earthly goods; nor does He ever promise that we will not encounter trials. Jeremiah 29:11-14 is not referring to an obscure faith economy in which our circumstances ebb and flow based on the level of belief we have in God. I've wanted a new Jeep Wrangler for years, but no matter how many times I tell God about how badly I want one, there are still those menacing car payments to deal with. His plans for our welfare have nothing to do with following the rules for success that our culture has created, but instead reside solely in the person of Jesus Christ. The riches that flow from the grace of God are enough to satisfy our longings, because it is in this grace that we find life itself.[9] Our heart idols are empty and powerless. We must repent of them and believe in the one true gospel to meet our every need.

Jeremiah 29:11 gives us hope that goes beyond our earthly circumstances. God declares His sovereignty and foreknowledge over each of us when He states, "For I know the plans I have for you..." It is an amazing comfort to know that God has gone before us and has formulated the plans that will be for our well-being, even if He does not literally promise to provide us with food, jobs, or shelter. This passage is not about achieving the plans or goals that we want to accomplish. It's pointing to the fact that long ago God orchestrated a plan that would benefit your welfare and give you a future with Him, birthed from the hope found in Jesus.

The sad reality is that in this broken world some of us will live our entire lives in strife and hardship. The rest of us may be successful and never have to face real turmoil. I do not know how our fates are determined, but I have to trust that no matter what life throws at me, there is a loving God who has a plan to redeem my life, even if that plan is not fully achieved by the time I breathe my last breath. For me, the Source of my

---

[9] Ephesians 2:7, 3:8; Colossians 2:2-3; Philippians 4:19;

success has nothing to do with this earthly existence or in anything that is prone to change over time. The only place where I have found this unimaginable fulfillment is in the promises of the gospel. To some that may seem like a simple or naive belief, but I take great comfort in knowing that with all of the evil that exists in this life, God is still in control. As Psalm 115:3 says, "Our God is in the heavens, and does all that He pleases." I don't think this is my way of putting my head in the sand, trying to ignore the atrocities of this world. What it does is free me from having to explain the unexplainable while trusting that God has been here since the beginning and knows considerably more than my finite mind can ever comprehend.

Whether Christ is pointing to the provision God gives to the birds and how much more important we are to Him than our feathered friends (Matthew 6:26) or Paul is urging us to stop stressing over things that we were never meant to be in control of in the first place (Philippians 4:6), Scripture is constantly reminding us that God wants to provide for our spiritual well-being. It may seem cruel that God would not always provide for our physical wants, but what I think is lost in our understanding of God is that He has provided us new and eternal life with Him. When our possessions have worn out, our house is in ruins, and our health has vanished, we will still possess the gift of being one with God. Christ has paved our road to the only success that matters with His sacrifice and nothing and no one can take that away from us. We no longer have to project worldly success or perform for the world's applause, because the cross of Christ was and remains all-sufficient.

If God desires to provide for us in Jesus, as well as provide for us on this earth, is it really a stretch to believe that God orchestrated social welfare programs? At the core of what these programs seek to provide lies the heart of God; in them we can see the redemptive story of the gospel. A sinful humanity will take the good things of God and make a mess of them up every time. So it's also not a stretch to argue that our welfare programs are broken because they are designed by, run by, and used by broken people. And yet the concept of helping people when they fall on hard times reflects the very nature of God. A desire to help the marginalized in society is what James 1:27 calls "pure religion." I have to believe that if there is nothing inside of us that desires to help other people, there is a great possibility that we have never met Jesus. When we encounter the pure love of Christ, a love for God and others should begin to manifest.

The United States Department of Agriculture publishes monthly statistics that show the average food costs for families in the US. According to the USDA, in April 2015 the suggested budget a family of four would need in order to pay for their groceries was between $1,062.92 and $1,287.87.[10] For most families, that is equivalent to an additional monthly mortgage or rent payment just to put food on the table. Given such staggering statistics, how can people of little economic means find hope? Maybe a better question is, how can the church help

---

[10] USDA, "Official USDA Food Plans..."

these families cultivate hope in the midst of such daunting realities?

A popular thing to do, especially in new church plants, is to try to capture the spirit of the "Acts 2 church." Acts 2 tells of the formation of the church after Christ had accomplished God's plan of salvation on the cross and ascended back to heaven. The first description of this earliest church is found in Acts 2: 42-47. Verses 42-43 reflect its communal aspect and its commitment dedication to the teachings of Christ. Verse 44 states, "And all who believed were together and had all things in common." In other words, the new church possessed a few basic attributes of the kind of faith that need to be cultivated if it is to seek the welfare of others.

The new converts were "together." They were engaged in each other's lives and were aware of each other's stories. What is striking about this verse is that "they had all things in common." The reason this is surprising to me is that the first church more than likely contained not just Jewish believers, but also "Gentiles" or non-Jewish people living under Roman authority, which would make for significant cultural differences. Let's say that they were all Jewish converts and shared a similar culture. It is reasonable to believe that even within this group there would still be different social and economic classes of people. Merchants, educators, craftsmen, and beggars were probably some of the demographics that were represented in the first churches. We see examples of beggars coming to faith in Christ (Mark 10:46-52) and believers buying large sums of land and donating the proceeds to the work of the church (Acts 4:34). Therefore the fact "they had all things in common" does not point to just their cultural similarities, but also to a collective understanding that all their "glorious riches" came from Christ which in turn freed them to see their material possessions and staples of life as things to be shared.

Verse 45 confirms this: "And they were selling their possessions and belongings and distributing the proceeds to all, as any had need." I am not arguing that the first Christians were socialists, but that for them accumulating wealth was meaningless compared to having received the gift of God's forgiveness. If churches today would seriously strive to emulate these New Testament principles, they could change the face of welfare in our country. I know that is an uncomfortable statement and maybe even an unfair one. However, I do believe the Bride of Christ could very well be the answer to the poverty dilemma that faces our world.

Now take a deep breath, because I don't believe that Scripture is telling you to put all your stuff on craigslist or orchestrate a liquidation garage sale. Acts 2 is not commanding all Christians to get rid of everything they have ever owned. We have to approach these passages not with strict pragmatism, but rather try to capture the spirit of what God is telling us. Acts 2 provides practical guidelines for cultivating a faith that seeks the welfare of other people. Before we assess a person's situation, we should first try to understand their unique story.

This only happens when we come "together" as a community.[11] It is only in community that relationships are formed and we become more inclined to do radical things with our resources for the sake of others.

Successful people in the US are the iconic moguls of our day; they set new trends for us to follow. I have to reiterate that there is nothing wrong with being successful, working hard, and enjoying what you have earned, as long as earthly success is not our sole or even primary source of happiness. Having a fruitful career and impacting the marketplace is fantastic. But if your only ambition is clawing your way to the top of the corporate ladder, then you will not see those who have fallen off the rungs.

I believe with everything inside of me that God has a plan, a plan that is focused on our eternal welfare. A plan that cleanses our souls and gives us hope. A plan that promises a future with Him. In response to that plan, we too can have a plan. A plan that puts us in a position to know people's stories, to be "together" with them during all the seasons of their life, to make disciples, and possibly to provide for their needs as a response to our needs having been met through the glorious riches of Christ.

Acts 2:47 states the first church members were "praising God and having favor with all the people." Being on food stamps was for us both humbling and beautiful. Because God

---

[11] In verses 44 and 46 both make it clear that the people of the first church were consistently gathering together and would frequently interact.

provided for us in that season, my entire family now seeks to provide for others spiritually, emotionally, and physically. When we seek the welfare of others, we can gain favor with them as they see us praising God for the gifts of benevolence that He has given us to steward. As we get to know them and become aware of their story, then we can share the hope that God has great plans for them. That sounds like a successful life to me.

I may never get to own a home and I am at peace with that now because my success in life is no longer attached to that idol. At the end of my days I want to be known as someone who helped others zealously, loved ferociously, and was content with what God had given me in Christ. My performance matters little when it comes to earning God's blessings. For Christ performed for me on the cross to which I am forever in His debt. There is truly only one success story we need to cling to which is the good news where Christ defeated sin and death once in for all. Never has a success story been such good news to all who hear and believe.

CHAPTER 5

Political Prophets

I love living in Oregon, but there are a few things I miss about the great state of Texas. The top three are family, friends, and enchiladas. As much as I love the Pacific Northwest, people here have yet to master the art of "Tex-Mex" and I am officially soliciting someone from the Lone Star State to come help remedy this problem. I promise to be your first and most loyal patron

The differences between living in the hippy bastion known as Oregon versus living in the state you're, as the Texas' slogan says, not supposed to mess with is staggering. In Oregon, it is totally acceptable to ask at a restaurant where your meat of choice was bred, raised, and butchered. In Texas the hardest question I used to have is what type of barbeque sauce I wanted to slather on my prey. In Portland your eatery has to advertise that your product is local, free-range, gluten-free, vegan, and fair trade if you want to keep your business afloat. In Texas I just wanted to know if the deep-fried deliciousness for dinner was going to give me cardiac issues before or after dessert.

Everything is really bigger in Texas and you have to love a state that has so much pride for the place they call home. Texas has big personalities and even bigger churches. Speaking of Texas churches, some also participate in an amazing phenomenon of advertisement known as church signs. This is where churches use the marque in front of their buildings to advertise their services or offer motorists a thoughtful passage from Scripture. This is not an exclusive Texas occurrence. Church signs can be seen throughout the Bible-belt, but the most interesting in my opinion seem to come from Texas. Often churches use their signs not to just inform the public about the latest potluck or conference, some also tend to promote pretty outlandish and some just plain crazy cultural notions.

My favorite church sign sayings deal with various topics and it seems to me the smaller the church, the more awkward their signs tend to be, such as the tiny church in north Fort Worth that told drivers heading to work, "Coffee is hot. Hell is hotter. God loves you alatte." I never thought coffee could be used as an evangelism tool, scare tactic, health warning, and pun at the same time. There was another church I used to pass on my way to teach at Dallas Baptist University that had a sign that revealed a warning that their blacktop was "for church parking only, violators will be baptized." Welcoming and informative. Nothing like getting your point across by threatening rule-breakers with forced participation in a holy sacrament.

There are even books filled with funny and awkward church signs that you can set on your coffee table and use as a conversation starter when guests drop by! Out of all the church signs I have witnessed, there is one church sign that has stuck with me for a very long time. It was November 2012, and the United States was on the cusp of re-electing its first African American President for another four years. The owners of the sign was a church in Dallas and they had a particularly interesting statement during that intense election year: "Jesus would vote Republican."

Now honestly this is not the most outlandish thing I have ever seen. Some of you may have just have given a hearty "amen" to the notion that Jesus would be an active member of the GOP. I can see why this church felt this way due to the convergence of evangelicalism and conservative politics, but to actually say that you truly believe Jesus would align Himself with one political party is not just untrue, it is extremely unhelpful for the cause of Christ. Every time I think of this sign I picture Jesus in a nice, dark blue designer suite with an American flag pinned to its lapel, kissing babies, and shaking the hands of His constituents.

I have taught college-level Political Science for several years. Most of my teaching has happened within the walls of private Christian universities. Each semester there seems to be an overarching theme that if I am a Christian, then there is no way I can support a liberal platform. It's hard to tell if right-wing conservatives have hijacked Christianity or if ultra-conservative Christians have taken over the Republican Party, but either way the result has been the creation of a political chasm in our country. These days "For God and country" go hand-in-hand, leaving us often wondering which should come first or if is there is even any separation between them anymore.

When I was in graduate school I was the only "conservative" in the entire program. When President George W. Bush won a second term in 2004, I took it as an excuse the following morning in my "History of the Presidents" class to gloat. I am not saying I now regret voting for Bush, but I was so entrenched in my beliefs that I forgot altogether that I was first a follower of Christ versus being a Republican. Thinking back on that time, it is surprising I had any friends whatsoever. I used to get into it with one particular colleague named Chad. I would spend countless hours accusing him of being a bleeding-heart liberal whose views on wealth redistribution would lead to the creation of a welfare state. Who would have thought that just a few years later I would need some of that redistributed wealth? Sorry, Chad! I was so fixated on a set of extra biblical principles that I ended up mistrusting government programs and especially our national assistance program. I never cared to understand what someone on government assistance was going through. I never cared to hear Chad's story and why he felt the way he did.

With great patience my peers in graduate school put up with me and my attitude. The issue was not that they did not respect my political beliefs; their greatest problem with me was that I had no interest in their views. I admit I loved the idea of being the maverick in the department and the tree-huggers worst nightmare, but in the end I made very little impact on my peers and simply confirmed their own prejudice that Christians were actually not very Christ-like. Let me state that there is nothing wrong with siding with one particular party when you're in the voting booth. I love politics and I love people who are passionate about their political beliefs. However, there is something very wrong if you claim to be a believer in Christ, yet your political brand trumps the name of the One who brought you into a right standing with the God of the universe.

This past semester one of my students asked me if I was a Democrat or Republican because he simply could not come to any clear conclusions based on my statements in class. I responded that I affiliate with the party of "it's complicated" and left him feeling bewildered. Since graduate school many things have happened that have softened my hardline stances, the most dramatic of which was God allowing me to go on government assistance. I still hold to conservative principles, but I have also gained more balance in my beliefs, while making sure that my politics never gets in the way of my mission of sharing the gospel with others. Going on welfare helped me to filter my opinions through the lens of Christ by letting me see how He views the hurting, the destitute, and the least of these. It has become the best political platform I have ever adopted. If we only depend on talking-heads, with perfect hair and a corporate profit-driven agenda for our "news," then we will never get to know the truth about our fellow, albeit less-fortunate, citizens.

It's really irrefutable that there is a culture war going on today between evangelicals and everyone else. With every issue that warrants national attention it seems that both sides run to social media in order to make sure they let everyone know their official position. The problem with participating in a culture war is that neither side wins. Instead they become deeper entrenched in their opinions until they are unwilling to even consider the other side's perspective.

When the two sides in a controversy refuse to see any merit in anyone's point of view except their own, what began as a civilized difference of opinion turns into fear-mongering, where one side tries to paint the opposition as a threat to the very fabric of civilization should they prevail. When we fear-monger, we are using a strategy that is intended to scare people into believing things that have nothing to do with the teachings of Jesus. When we choose to think the worst of others, we create silos, fan the flames of anger, and marginalize people simply because we disagree with them.

Time and time again I see pastors on social media making claims that if certain legislation does or does not pass, God will turn His back on the United States. Such statements imply that God is not sovereign and may even be surprised by certain outcomes. On the contrary, God knows who is going to win the next election, because He wills it so. As I previously mentioned, Psalms 115:2-3 states, "Why should the nations say, 'Where is their God?' Our God is in the heavens; he does all that he pleases." This verse is comforting while also being somewhat terrifying, for despite all our planning and scheming, we are not in control. God is. The future we aspire to is not within our power to attain no matter how hard we try. James 4:14 states, "...yet you do not know what tomorrow will bring. What is your life? For you are a mist that appears for a little time and then vanishes." We are simply finite beings humbly clinging to the promises of an infinite God who is leading us on a path to eternal hope in His presence.

So let's go back to the church that touted Jesus as a Republican. What they are saying is that they care about promoting their political beliefs more than they care about sharing their church's hope in Christ. They may as well just put up a sign that says certain types of people are not welcome in their church. The implication would be that anyone who is searching for God, but whose politics may be a little progressive, should not give this church a second look.

The Jesus-is-a-Republican sign was soon taken down. I suppose someone complained, but unfortunately the damage had already been done. The sign may be gone, but the people who put it up remain the same. For as long as there are people who feel safe only when they surround themselves with others who believe exactly as they do, there will always be churches that encourage them in this false gospel. We have stereotyped ourselves politically and spiritually to the detriment of gospel effectiveness. It seems each year another social or political issue thickens the wall that divides evangelicals from the rest of society. I used to look forward to the campaign season because of the wonderful debates that would occur. Now I dread it because I know I will have to be an apologist for Jesus to my non-believing friends when politicians who ascribe to being a Christian say things that are very un-Christ like.

I would never ask anyone to give up their political beliefs. In fact, I would say that once people have a really solid grasp of what they believe, they should fight for those beliefs. That is what makes our democracy amazing. However, if you are a follower of Christ, your political stances must never override the mission of making disciples for Christ, because if you do, then you become just another casualty in the culture war.

We are all impacted by various socialization factors. Media, friends, family, education, and culture all play a huge role in how we see the world. But these should be secondary to allowing Christ to define our worldview. However, so many Christians have a skewed understanding of what a Christian worldview actually involves. Campaigning for the gospel requires a greater conviction than any political campaign regardless of the issues at stake. Though some of these issues may be linked to Scriptural truths, we must give priority to the cause of Christ before we move on to other platforms.

Right now as I write this sentence, we as a country are gearing up to see (more than likely) Donald Trump and Hilary Clinton battle it out for the most powerful job in the world. I never thought the former First Lady and the billionaire reality TV star would be in this position, but here we are unless some underdog can unseat them in the primary. I can't say that the 2015-2016 primary season has not been entertaining, but it has also brought us at what I feel is an all-time low for our country.

There has so much hate spewed from both sides that it leaves one to wonder if there is really any hope left in our political system. The battle lines are clearer than ever now and there seems to be no place for those stuck in the middle.

We act sometimes as if those who oppose us politically, spiritually, or philosophically are less than human. We watch as our politicians demean each other all the while smiling and touting their faith in Christ. Where have we lost the deep desire to help people, to compromise, to engage, and to care more for the character of the person before us, not their outward persona? I want to suggest that in the face of opposition, particularly in times like these where our country is so divided over a host of issues, there is a prime opportunity to show the love of Christ.

In Romans 12:9-21, Paul gives us a roadmap on how we should treat others in the church, as well as, those who stand in opposition of us. Verses 9-13 speak on holding on to, "genuine love" and to show, "brotherly affection" to those in the church. Genuine love is love that comes without strings attached and does not look for something in return. Brotherly affection is a heart position where see others in the church as actual family where we treat them as if they were related to us. Paul continues to urge us to be patient when hard times come, be zealous in serving God, and to not just show, but seek out opportunities to show hospitality.

In verse 14-21 Paul shifts focus from how believers should treat each other to how Christ-followers are to treat others outside of the faith. Paul makes one of the most counter-cultural statements found in the New Testament when he says that we should bless our enemies, serve those who would oppose us, and to live in harmony with others. I know that can be difficult because people are difficult. Yet we find strength and the desire to help those who we find in opposition to us because we were helped when we were in opposition to God. Before Christ, we are in complete defiance towards God and our lives are similar to mud-slinging political ads that slander our Creator. However, God pursued us anyway. People are messy. You are messy still, yet that should not hold you back from seeking out the welfare of those who are on the other side of the cultural battlefront.

To repeat what I've said earlier, we are all impoverished people. No matter how much we have in our bank account, sin has made paupers of us all. Therefore when we seek the welfare of others, we are seeking the welfare of all humanity, no matter what their cultural or political beliefs may be. Yet time and time again the church alienates groups of people based on their differences and excludes them from the work of the Kingdom.

When I was a kid in the late 80s and early 90s, Christians who had gone through a divorce were the lepers of the church. They were outcasts, shunned from contributing to the mission of Christ, and treated as sub-humans. When I was in graduate school my wife and I met Rex and Becky Cooper, a wonderful couple in their 50s who had been married for about 10 years. For both of them this was their second marriage. Both their previous spouses had left them. The Coopers still to this day have one of the most amazing marriages I have ever seen, and their mutual love for Jesus overflows to those around them. They taught my wife and me so much about working through conflict, what grace looked like in a marriage, and how to love one another with the heart of Christ.

I don't advocate for divorce, I am just advocating for people, God's most precious Creation. There must be grace for those whose lives have played out differently from our own. Becky and Rex did not wish for their first marriages to end in divorce, but they were able to take an unfortunate turn in their lives and use it for the glory of God. They continue to this day to help young couples cultivate Christ-centered marriages that can stand the trials of this world. They are saints and do not allow their past to hinder their ministry today.

Seeking the welfare of others cannot happen until we start fighting for their hearts and minds on behalf of Christ. Jesus often engaged people who were politically and/or culturally His opponents.[12] But that did not stop Him from seeing past who they were and what they had done. Christ knew that through faith in Him their past could be erased and they could start to become all that God had intended for their lives.

In Luke 10 there is a story that is pretty familiar among church folk known as the parable of the Good Samaritan. Jesus had sent out 72 of his disciples to go to the nearby cities and minister in His name. They returned telling tales of all the amazing things God had done in their midst. He is then

---

[12] John 4:1-44, John 4:45-54. Note also that Paul's entire ministry was focused on the Gentiles who had almost nothing in common with his Jewish background.

approached by a lawyer (a lawyer joke here would be just too easy) who is looking to justify his feelings of ill-will towards people in general.

Like many who want to justify their sinful behavior, the lawyer begins by asking a question that he more than likely knows the answer to, but he is hoping that Jesus will offer him a legal loophole that will resolve his quandary. In verse 25 he asks of Jesus, "Teacher, what shall I do to inherit eternal life?" Since Jesus is God it was obvious to Him that He was being tested. Just like many of us who love our prejudices more than God, this lawyer was seeking to justify the sin that resided in his heart.

Jesus begins by asking him what was written in the Law that God had given the people of Israel through Moses. The lawyer knows his Scripture and quotes Deuteronomy 6:5 which states, "You shall love the Lord your God with all your heart and with all your soul and with all your strength and with all your mind, and your neighbor as yourself." Christ affirms the lawyer's answer and seems to end the conversation by saying, "Do this, and you will live." Christ is telling him that if you truly love God then you will also love the One who is the incarnate God and this love will lead you to love others. It is our pursuit to fall more deeply in love with God because that will ultimately cause us to love one another. People are messy and difficult to love, especially if all we have to offer them is our imperfect human love. That is why loving people who are different from ourselves requires the love that we have received through Christ. Simple enough. However, the lawyer then tries to trip

Jesus up by abruptly asking Him in verse 29, "Who is my neighbor?"

Jesus immediately begins to tell the parable of a Jew who was walking to Jericho when he was attacked by robbers and left for dead. Two fellow Jews (a priest and a Levite) come upon the man, see that he is in dire straits, but decide not to stop and help him despite certainly being familiar with Deuteronomy 6:5 which the lawyer had just quoted. Then the hero of the story, a Samaritan, comes by and takes pity on the beaten traveler, takes him to the nearest town, and pays for him to be nursed back to health.

Jews despised Samaritans because they were a mixed race, half-Assyrian and half-Jewish. By the time of Christ the Samaritans generally believed in God and the writings of Moses, while rejecting the other prophetic writings. Because of this, Jews despised Samaritans more so than even their Roman oppressors.

The obvious lesson of this parable is that we are to care for those in need without legalism or prejudice towards anyone who need help. What is most fascinating to me is the lawyer's implicit question in asking Jesus to define the meaning of "neighbor." "Whose welfare must I care about and whose can I dismiss? Who are not worthy of my attention? What cultural, ethical, or racial attributes must people have that will justify me not having to help them in their time of need?" He's thinking, "Come on, Jesus! You know there are certain people who aren't worth our time!"

Christ could have argued the meaning of Deuteronomy 6:5, exegete the text, and come up with three points in the fashion of a perfect Baptist sermon. Instead, He immediately launches into a controversial yet powerful parable which points to an important lesson of how loving God with all our hearts should give us the ability to crush all of our prejudices towards people and liberate us to care for them. Jesus uses a man whose very existence is offensive to Jews to show them that Samaritan have a greater capacity for displaying God's love than many of the racially pure children of Abraham.

So who is your neighbor? Is it just people who agree with you politically? Is it just people who believe that global warming is a myth? Is it just those who have never been on welfare? It is easy to "love your neighbor as yourself" when your neighbor stands on the same side of the cultural divide as you do. It is much more difficult to love people who not only march to the beat of a different drum, but bring the rest of the orchestra with them.

The Samaritan in Jesus' parable did not see a Jew, but rather a fellow human being who needed help. I pray that we will see more groups to claim Jesus as their Lord begin to engage those who disagree with them, that they will seek to love them as Christ loves them. This hope extends beyond the realm of secular culture. What must people think about the gospel when they see so much inter-church fighting, so many denominational skirmishes, and pastor-superstar quarrels? We must focus again on loving our neighbors by sharing with them and living out the gospel which can mend all wounds.

In this time of racial tension, growing economic disparity, and urban gentrification, the church must be the consistent voice of hope amid so much turmoil. If we want to impact our communities, we should not separate ourselves from the culture, but rather bring Jesus to the table of ideas. So often evangelicals think it's more important to defeat their political and cultural opponents than it is to win the war for their eternal souls.

When it comes to expressing differences, it's acceptable to admit you do not understand what others are feeling. I once attended an amazing Christian conference on adoption in Seattle. At the time my wife and I were preparing to adopt our precious nine-year-old son Duo who is Chinese, and I felt a workshop on diversity and multicultural families would be beneficial. The speaker was excellent, but I think everyone was caught off-guard when the workshop turned into a question-and-answer symposium full of blunt realities.

The conversations were raw, and yet people of all races were very gracious. One woman admitted she did not know any African Americans, and yet was in the process of adopting an African American boy. Another parent admitted his fear of bringing up racial issues in public out of concern that he would be labeled a racist. A Latino woman told a moving story of trying to teach her children to not believe all the stereotypes that non-Latinos have hoisted upon their culture. At one point I looked around the room and felt as if I was glimpsing what heaven will be like. Here were people from all walks of life who were one in Christ and who desired to glorify Him for all eternity. They desired knowledge so that knowledge could turn into understanding and love.

The first step in learning about people who are different than us is in confessing that we do not have a complete understanding of what they go through on a daily basis. Too often we make false assumptions about them or just impose our own values upon them. Admitting that we do not understand everything about people of different races, lifestyles, or politics is not a sign of ignorance, but a sign of humility especially when that's coupled with a desire to understand how they perceive the world. Presuming that we already know all that there is to know about people who are different than us is not only arrogance, but it can also be harmful to the gospel.

Jesus is the great equalizer. He offers us hearts that long to connect with people who are different than ourselves. The gospel is not the property of one particular group, and Jesus is not the Lord of only certain select individuals. Jesus is the One we must follow and identify with over and above every other human characteristic or distinguishing feature.

More than that, when we put others first, when we seek with God's help to be a good neighbor to everyone without favoritism, we bring glory to God. As Paul states in Romans 15:5-7, "May the God of endurance and encouragement grant you to live in such harmony with one another, in accord with Christ Jesus, that together you may with one voice glorify the God and Father of our Lord Jesus Christ. Welcome one another as Christ has welcomed you, for the glory of God."

When your side wins a political victory, does that allow you disparage dismiss those on the losing side? When a verdict goes your way, does that allow you to mock those who sought a different outcome? When a particular group of people is shown in an unflattering light, do we assume that it must be an accurate stereotype? Sometimes being "right" on an issue is not worth sacrificing the harmony we have with others in Christ, especially when we later realize we were wrong all along.

Jesus did not lead a political party, but He was a revolutionary who challenged every form of prejudice that stood in the way of people being restored to a right relationship first with the Father and then to one another. The welfare of our neighbors should be of vital concern to those of us who love God and follow Jesus. People are messy and sometimes their opinions make them even messier to deal with. But we should never allow someone's politics, lifestyle, economic status, or anything else ever inhibit us from helping them in times of need. It's not about trying to change everything about them; it's about sharing how their hearts can be changed forever by the gospel.

Finally, I have one last thought for my Republican friends whom I love so dearly. When Jesus made His triumphant entry into Jerusalem, He wasn't riding on an elephant...

CHAPTER 6

If I Had A Million Dollars

One of my all-time favorite bands is Counting Crows. I used to jam (for Millennials, that means "listen to excessively") to their album *August and Everything After* as if it contained the theme songs for my life. In college I got to hear them play live. It was a fantastic concert. One of the best parts of the show was not only Adam Duritz's amazing dreadlocks, but the band that opened for Counting Crows. They were a pleasant surprise.

I was familiar with this Canadian band even though they have an incredibly awkward name. They were a perfect mid-90s sensation who were extremely underrated lyrical geniuses at infusing their songs with pop-cultural commentary. "Be My Yoko Ono" referred to John Lennon's wife breaking up the Beatles, and "Brian Wilson" was about the misfortunes of the former Beach Boy. They also are further proof that many good things do come out of Canada!

The band has one funny song entitled, "If I had a Million Dollars," basically the song is about a list of things that a guy would buy for his lady if he had extravagant wealth. It's a catchy nonsense song that makes fun of the super wealthy. One line at the end of each chorus is, "If I had a million dollars, I'd buy your love." Now even though this song is ridiculous, that line is an interesting concept.

I'm sure we would agree that we cannot buy someone's love per se, but there is nothing inherently wrong in buying people gifts as a way to show them our appreciation, love, or respect. One of my favorite things is buying presents for my wife. I know she feels loved when I surprise her with a small token of my appreciation. However, my wife's love for me is not dependent on her receiving gifts from me or our kids. She does not calculate how much we love her based on the quality of the gifts we give her (thank goodness). My wife's love for us is birthed out of Christ's unconditional love for her. And a good thing too, because she has a table that I bought for her that used to have four legs until I broke one of them. For two years I have vowed to fix it, and I've promised I will before our youngest reaches college.

When it comes right down to it, I would bet that most people would rather have an extravagant relationship than an extravagant gift. With the proper and sometimes costly care and attention, relationships will endure, unlike so many lesser things like tables. In our greatest triumphs or our worst defeats, it is our relationships that make life truly meaningful. Deep relationships are simply priceless.

In the church we often launch capital campaigns to raise money for a new building program or for making repairs to existing structures. I am not against church buildings, even large church buildings. I think people are being somewhat narrow-minded in opposing a building project without considering the positive impact that having an established space in the community can have. I know many pastors and congregations are anti-buildings, but these sacred spaces can be utilized for gospel renewal and produce a retreat for the weary.

It's how we see the functionality and purpose of these facilities that makes the difference. We must define our needs versus our wants. I understand the need of building a children's wing so that the next generation of believers can hear the gospel in a safe environment. But does the church really need to pay for the slides that kids shoot down to get to those classes? I mean don't get me wrong, that would be the really cool to see kids zipping down static chutes of fun to their Sunday school class, but this feature is probably not practical.

Unfortunately, many churches believe that the more money they spend on brick and mortar, the more people they can entice to follow God. That's kind of like a "Field of Dreams" strategy, but instead of Kevin Costner it's Jesus whispering to the pastor, "If you build it, they will come." I have been in meetings where pastors seemed more passionate about their buildings than those who fill them up each Sunday. Are we trying to buy the love of our parishioners and their friends? On a side note, if your pastor is having a quiet time in Nehemiah, be prepared for a capital campaign to follow in the coming months.

I have talked to church staff members who see the proliferation of new buildings in their community, coupled with displays of cutting-edge technology, as a call on their church to "keep up with the times" if they hope to stay relevant. In some ways they are correct. Churches need to have structures that keep pace with the culture of their community, but they should not feel pressured to spend millions of dollars on décor and the latest technologies. The church is not a building or a brand name but a bride. The structure should promote the overwhelming hope we have in Christ and not get caught up in how many seats the worship center can hold.

There are plenty of books out now that speak of the plague of consumerism within the church and within the psyche of the American evangelical. I could never do the topic justice as I still have poor consumer habits that disqualify me from being an expert on the subject. I can't come from a place of wisdom when the baristas at my local coffee shop can recognize my voice over the drive-thru intercom. That said, being on food stamps did give me a different perspective on how we spend our money both as individuals and as the body of Christ. For so long I thought we (believers) could entice those far from God by spending money on exterior attractions, that if we just dangled something new and shiny in front of their eyes, they'd hopefully take the bait. However, now that we are past our season of being on welfare, I am convinced that investing in people and relationships is better than any baubles or trinkets we can offer them. I am no expert on how to help churches maximize their spending power, but I do know what it feels like to be on welfare and be surrounded by a consumer society.

One of the key things God taught my wife and me while on welfare is that what we produce needs to outweigh what we consume. That obviously impacts spending habits. Basic economics tells us that in order to stay afloat financially, we must have more money coming in than going out. No one can keep on spending more than they have coming in and expect to make it. And yet as disciples of Christ, at times we are called on to violate this simple principle and give away more than we take in.

Maybe churches or church people want to help, but don't have any money themselves. I get that. But maybe it's time for churches and individual members to start asking why they can't afford it. Is it because some value buildings over people, comfort over tension, programs over participants, recognition over impact? I keep asking myself where and how I need to change my habits. Am I consuming more than I am producing? If so, how did I get to this point, and what might God be calling me to do better?

Jesus had no money, and yet what He had He gave away for the sake of others, including His life. In Matthew 25 Christ begins to explain to His disciples the final judgment and what it looks like to be a child of God. He says that when He returns people will be separated into two groups, those who love God (the sheep), and those who do not (the goats). For this very reason is why I keep sheep and not goats on my farm! Christ then makes a startling statement, that those who are the children of God gave Him food when He was hungry, drink when He was thirsty, clothing when He was naked, company when He was in prison, and care when He was sick. Likewise those who did not do these things for Him cannot be children of God.

Not surprisingly, the disciples can't recall any time when Jesus was in any of these situations. His response in verses 45-46 is both powerful and terrifying: "Then he will answer them, saying, 'Truly, I say to you, as you did not do it to one of the least of these, you did not do it to me.' And these will go away into eternal punishment, but the righteous into eternal life."

Christ is not saying that if those who never come to the aid of a homeless person are doomed to an eternal separation from God. But what He is doing is describing a mindset and a heart position that all of His followers must have. Just as He gave up everything including His life for our sakes, so we too ought to give our lives for the sake of others. If there is not one tiny urge inside us to serve the "least of these" then we have to ask ourselves if we really have met Jesus. Not just those who have no money or a roof over their head, but also the poor in spirit, and those emotionally and spiritually bankrupt. Jesus commands us to love God with all our being and to love our neighbor to the same extent that God has shown His love for us (Matthew 22:39). Anyone claiming to be a Christian who is indifferent to these words and commands I believe needs to wrestle with the possibility that they do not really believe in Jesus or have been introduced to a counterfeit version of the Messiah.

Modern evangelicalism is constantly trying to buy the love of people by spending millions of dollars on trying to make them feel more comfortable or relevant. Christ on the other hand is telling His disciples in Matthew 25 that it is the marginalized, the outcast, the socially ostracized, and the impoverished who need our attention. The act of serving the "least of these" is in itself a picture of how Christ serves us. Because of sin we are all diminished, we are all in a position of need. Money cannot save us. Only the attention, care, and sacrifice that Christ provides can transform the lost into children of God.

With all the wealth that we as the church lavish on ourselves, it seems odd to me that we would not feel compelled to splurge on the least of these. I think we often forget how spiritually impoverished we once were because we may have never experienced material poverty or the idea that souls can also be impoverished is a foreign concept. It is only when we realize that we too are the "least of these" that we will feel compelled to act because in one way or another, we are all in desperate need.

One of the most marginalized groups of people in the Bible (and some would say even in modern times) were orphans. When my family began to fundraise towards our first adoption, the one thing we constantly asked ourselves was, "How are we going to pay for this?" Our adoption cost us over $30,000, and given our limited resources, this seemed an unimaginable mountain to overcome. However, God, as He so often does, showed my wife and me who really owns all the wealth in the world. As people became aware of our financial need, we were overwhelmed by the countless friends and family members who helped make the adoption possible. In the end God raised every penny we needed and kept us from going into debt.

Two things happened during this amazing time that I will never forget. First, in the nine months it took to raise the money and complete the adoption process, our kids scraped and saved every penny to put towards the adoption. Whether it was birthdays, holidays, chores, and any other means by which a kid acquires cash, my children gave all they received to make the adoption possible. We had a large mason jar on our mantle and from time to time the kids would fill it with their earnings. Even when we gave them the option of spending the money on themselves, they refused every time. My kids showed me what it means to invest in someone instead of something.

The second thing happened while my wife and I were in China to finalize the adoption. The day came to exchange the dollars we had brought with us for Chinese Yuan. When we handed the bank teller $10,000 in cash, she had a nervous smile on her face and quickly went to get her manager. They brought out two large counting machines. It took about 30 minutes to complete the process and we sat in amazement while a multitude of colorful currency came rushing out of these machines. Then it struck me. As the Yuan shot out, I "saw" Jude's birthday money, Noah's chore money, and Evy's Christmas cash. I "saw" Kristen's, sacrificial gift to our adoption. She's a friend of ours who holds down two nursing jobs to make rent. I "saw" Judy Stalling's hard-earned money making an impact on the other side of the world. She's my former drama teacher. I "saw" the Hollifields', the Hawkins', the Singletons', the Woodruffs' the Bassetts', and countless other families' hard-earned money that they had given away to rescue a child. These dear friends and many others, heard a call to help "the least of these" and responded out of love for the God who had rescued them.

Why can we not, as the church, do something radical with our resources? Maybe some of us need to evaluate rather or not we are consuming more than we are producing. Maybe our contribution does not necessarily have to take the form of financial assistance. Maybe our contribution is to love people for who they are, acknowledging where they have been, and caring for where they are headed. We don't need a million dollars to buy the love of others. Christ has already purchased our love and we could never fathom the cost. That love is a great investment to be spread around, and one that will always pay off in the end.

CHAPTER 7

The Least of Us

I once saw in downtown Portland a man riding a unicycle, dressed in a leisure suit, wearing a Darth Vader mask covering his head, and playing the bagpipes. It was not a gimmick for a local eatery and he was not asking for money. For this mobile Scottish *Star Wars* enthusiast, this was just his everyday self-expression. Among the citizenry of Portland, this type of spectacle is fairly common, and some would even say expected. Jesus is kind of like that too. In the eyes of those who do not know or understand Him, He is often seen as a gimmick or a spectacle, while for those who do, He can become nothing out of the ordinary.

Some Christians want to turn Jesus into a spectacle and are often successful. They use Him to push their own agendas or to justify their sinful behaviors. Some try to find Jesus in the deep emotional events of their lives, as they search for some kind of "a ha" moment that will prove that there actually is a Messiah. However, I tend to find Jesus most often showing up in the mundane and simple situations of life. It's in the everyday that Christ reveals to us how much we are loved, that thanks to Him we wake up every morning, we are free, we are safe, and we are alive in His presence one more day. Jesus showed up in a big way during our season on welfare, but that was less a mountaintop experience in our walk with Him, than it was a starting point in a beautiful, growing relationship.

Having to go on assistance is by no means the worst thing that can happen to someone, and our story is probably similar to other families who've had to do the same thing. In some regards our story is mild compared to a majority of the welfare society. However, as I have mentioned previously, God provided a healthy gospel perspective during this time that let us see Jesus as the great provider and that in light of His provision, we are to seek the welfare of others. From this gospel perspective we have discovered some rhythms that we try to be in step with as we maneuver through the waters of sanctification.

One of those rhythms is to be driven by grace and respond with mercy. Having a merciful mindset was always a struggle for me before going on government assistance. When I was younger I felt entitled, privileged, and superior to most people I encountered. My initial response when I saw a panhandler, a homeless person, or someone our culture had marginalized was to perceive immediately the issues that had led them to this sorry place and then compose their life's story in my head right there on the spot. Now, I tend not to make assumptions about people, but instead try to give others respect, dignity, and opportunity that has been afforded to me. Behind that unkempt face, the hard exterior, or the unbreakable gaze I see someone who is in obvious need of help.

Mercy always triumphs over judgment (James 2:13). When we act as judge we supplant God's sole right to judge, and our judgment, unlike His, is influenced by evil. I am not saying that we should not show discernment, but that we need to stop trying to play God by disparaging others. There is no twelve-step program to becoming more merciful. Mercy is birthed by the grace that God shows us daily; it's a continual pursuit of loving Jesus to our fullest. It is our response to a merciful Jesus who invites us into something better for our lives.

Another rhythm that has surfaced more in our lives in recent years is practicing, accepting, asking, and walking in forgiveness. It takes courage to admit when we are wrong, and yet Christ never intended for us to live weighed down by an anchor of guilt around our necks that constantly reminds us of past sins. Gospel forgiveness is immediate, and yet we often feel as if we still need to prove our worthiness to Jesus. It is true that God alone is worthy and holy and perfect, and we are not. But He loved us too much to allow us to carry the guilt of our sins for all eternity. His forgiveness freed us from the snares of our past, and we need to learn to live and love accordingly

We will have missteps in this life and at times we will find ourselves in the familiar territory of past sins. But God is not some tinkerer of the fates who has left us to our own devices while He sits back in His cosmic lounge chair watching to see how our lives will play out. He is there when times are good and there when hope has gone. God also does not desire us to exist in isolation. He will send others to intersect our lives for a season to remind us that we are not alone. These people will come with their different situations, backgrounds, and philosophies, and many will come for just a moment. These are our neighbors, family members, and other fellow humans who are trying to figure this whole thing out just as you are. So be kind. We all are winging it in some sense. Some are just better at hiding it. We all need to practice true repentance, the type of repentance that leads to joy while shaping us to be more like Jesus and less like our old sinful selves.

One rhythm that seems to come easier the older I get is having a sense of constant longing and desperation for God. When I walk away from Him I want to feel like I am underwater so that I instantly realize how much I need to get back to His presence so I can breathe again. I want to make a scene of intense worship when I encounter His Spirit and feel content resting in His presence. I want to always be in a position where I am able to grasp that my welfare is of great importance to my Creator and that I am known by Him as a father knows his child.

When our hearts have this deeper longing for God's presence, we often will find that it becomes more of a joy than a burden to follow God's commandments. We stop seeing the Bible as a list of rules designed to steal our joy, but instead we see His Word as God's invitation to something better. We stop feeling we're missing out on the "good" things of life, and start feeling more complete knowing that He is leading to a far more satisfying life.

There is a particular instance in Luke 7 starting in verse 36 where Jesus is hanging out with a Pharisee (your typical legalistic, pretentious, and religious zealot) named Simon. Simon had invited Jesus to a meal and the story picks up where Jesus is breaking bread with some upstanding religious elites of the day while, as was the custom, lying on the His side with His head towards the table. Out of nowhere "a woman of the city" who "was a sinner" burst onto the scene and began to anoint Jesus' dirty, road-weary feet with some expensive ointment and washing them with her tears and wiping them with her hair. More than likely the woman was a prostitute and in those days for someone of her social position to touch a religious leader, even more so a prophet, would have been taboo.

We do not know why this woman was in this lifestyle, but it's clear she was desperate to get out. Simon then turned to one of his scoffing peers and stated in verse 39, "If this man were a prophet, he would have known who and what sort of woman this is who is touching him, for she is a sinner."

Simon recognized this woman for who she was because he probably had seen her around the city or knew of her reputation. He immediately disdained her because she was obviously a "sinner" and maybe an unstable one at that. Without hesitation he wanted to denounce this lowly person to his religious friends in case they had any wrong ideas that he was condoning the scene playing out before them. Simon accused Jesus of not seeing this woman for who she really was, he was also casting doubt over whether Jesus was in fact the Messiah.

Many times I have preached this sermon and wondered aloud if we too sometimes act like a bunch of Simons when we are so quick to condemn those around us who have run into misfortune or made bad decisions. But now I tend to see myself more like the prostitute than Simon. I realize more clearly how I have prostituted my faith by engaging in material comforts, criticism of others, ego-driven projects, ideas of grandeur, and feelings of failure. I have pursued worldly success while putting a "use as needed" label on Jesus. Going on welfare was the moment I burst in on Jesus and began to sob at His feet, desperate for forgiveness.

Jesus responded to Simon and other men at this dinner party with a parable. He told them about a moneylender who had two people in his debt. One owed 500 denari (or about $500,000) and the other 50 denari (or about $5,000). When neither could pay, the moneylender canceled both their debts. Jesus then asked Simon in verse 42, "...now which one will love him more?" Simon said it was obviously the one with the larger debt. Jesus affirms His answer and then drives home an amazing point. Starting in verse 44, we read, "Then turning toward the woman he [Jesus] said to Simon, 'Do you see this woman? I entered your house; you gave me no water for my feet, but she has wet my feet with her tears and wiped them with her hair. You gave me no kiss, but from the time I came in she has not ceased to kiss my feet. You did not anoint my head with oil, but she has anointed my feet with ointment. Therefore

I tell you, her sins, which are many, are forgiven—for she loved much. But he who is forgiven little, loves little.'"

What I love about this passage is that Jesus is talking to Simon, but never takes His gaze off the woman. This message is not just for Simon, but for her as well, because she saw herself correctly as one of the least of these, and that Jesus was her only hope of redemption. For all his religious knowledge, Simon did not recognize Jesus for who He was and therefore failed to give Him the honor He was due. But this lowly woman somehow believed in Him and worshiped Him as best she knew how. She washed His feet with tears of repentance, and she anointed Him as the King who had come to conquer her bleak situation.

Many people will spend their entire lives seated at the head of their own table of self-righteousness shooing away anyone who makes them feel uncomfortable. But who will we identify with? The Simons of this world or the least of these? Will we come alongside these broken souls, or will we watch from the sidelines, wondering why Jesus would degrade Himself by rolling around in the muck of their lives?

I was once at the head of the table, feeling I had earned that seat of privilege. What I did not realize at the time was that life and purpose are found not at the head of the table, but at the feet of Jesus, begging for forgiveness from so many sins. Christ welcomes sinner and saint alike into His presence so that around the table of mercy we will find life.

This portion of Scripture is not saying that people with more baggage in their lives will appreciate what Jesus has to offer more than those who with less baggage. Jesus is inviting all of us to understand that all of us have much to be forgiven of and we have much to worship.

Everyone is in need of the One who will redeem us from our hopeless situation, worshiping ourselves, and giving our hearts away to the most seductive suitors. When we really understand the gospel and the nature of Jesus we will truly identify with this woman who so desperately needed salvation. On the other side of salvation we find ourselves under grace, practicing repentance, encouraged by forgiveness, and longing for more of the One who has altered our welfare forever.

My family finally got off welfare after my job situation took a turn for the better. We said goodbye to government forms and offices, as well as, that shiny food stamp card. I had a personal disposal ceremony for that card, but that's another story for another time. We were able to get back on our feet, afford our own groceries, and was able to leave the days of government assistance behind us. However, I do not look back at that season on welfare as a negative experience and in fact I thank God for allowing us to not just experience it, but survive it. I am the least of these, but the least of us is who God pursues.

I am not advocating that anyone in need of Jesus should go on welfare. That would be ridiculous and horrifying. Nor do I expect anyone to rush out to start some social justice initiative, successfully end world hunger, or reform our country's current political monster. I also do not desire for anyone to feel ashamed over how many times they did not give their spare change to the beggar they passed by. These actions are not the point of this book.

The words you have read are my confession, wrapped in random stories that seem to trail off at times. Thank you for enduring. I want so badly for you to meet the Jesus who was reintroduced to me in such an unexpected way. I hope your encounter with Christ will be as freeing as mine has been, and that your heart is forever comforted by the fact that He has changed your welfare forever. I hope for you also a new or renewed awareness of the fact that you now have a commission to seek the welfare of other people. With that knowledge, things can change for all of us who humbly see ourselves as being among the "least of these."

The gospel is truly good news and makes kings out of beggars. However, that good news was costly. Thankfully, we have a God who was willing to pay the price and allow us wanderers to come on home where there will always be a place for us at the table. So where do we begin? Quite honestly I am not all too sure, but I know each of us who long to follow Christ will eventually find our welfare faith.

Bibliography

Food Research and Action Center, "SNAP still matters for millions of people across the US" Food Research and Action Center, Accessed February 2, 2015, http://frac.org/reports-and-resources/snapfood-stamp-monthly-participation-dat

Siefert, Jeremy, *Dive!,* Documentary, Jeremy Siefert, 2010, Compeller Pictures, Los Angeles: 2011, DVD.

USDA, "Official USDA Food Plans: Cost of Food at Home at Four Levels, US Average" USDA, Accessed March 3, 2015, http://www.cnpp.usda.gov/sites/default/files/CostofFood Mar2015.pdf

About the Author

Kyle Raney lives in the Pacific Northwest and is involved in ministry in the capacity of pastor, speaker, and missionary. Kyle is married to his wonderful wife, Cassie, they have seven children who create the beautiful chaos that is their lives.

About Urban Loft Publishers

Urban Loft Publishers focuses on ideas, topics, themes, and conversations about all-things *urban*. Urban, or the city, is the central theme and focus for what we publish. In light of rapid urbanization and dense globalization comes the need to continue to hammer out a theology of the city, as well as the impetus to adapt and model urban ministry to the changing twenty-first century city. It is our intention to continue to mix together urban ministry, theology, urban planning, architecture, transportation planning, and the social science as we push the conversation forward about *renewing the city*. While we lean heavily in favor towards scholarly and academic works, we also explore the fun and light side of cities as well. Welcome to the *new* urban world.

www.urbanloftpublishers.com // @the_urban_loft

www.ingramcontent.com/pod-product-compliance
Lightning Source LLC
LaVergne TN
LVHW051420080426
835508LV00022B/3171